Books from Allworth Press

The Copyright Guide by Lee Wilson (softcover, 6 × 9, 192 pages, $18.95)

The Patent Guide by Carl W. Battle (softcover, 6 × 9, 224 pages, $18.95)

Legal-Wise: Self-Help Legal Guide for Everyone,
Third Edition by Carl W. Battle (softcover, 8½ × 11, 208 pages, $18.95)

Your Living Trust and Estate Plan: How to Maximize Your Family's Assets and Protect Your Loved Ones by Harvey J. Platt
(softcover, 6 × 9, 256 pages, $14.95)

Immigration Questions and Answers, Revised Edition by Carl R. Baldwin
(softcover, 6 × 9, 176 pages, $14.95)

Hers: The Wise Woman's Guide to Starting a Business on $2,000 or Less by Carol Milano (softcover, 6 × 9, 224 pages, $16.95)

Licensing Art and Design, Revised Edition by Caryn R. Leland
(softcover, 128 pages, $16.95)

The Internet Research Guide by Timothy K. Maloy
(softcover, 6 × 9, 208 pages, $18.95)

The Internet Publicity Guide by V. A. Shiva
(softcover, 6 × 9, 208 pages, $18.95)

The Writer's Legal Guide by Tad Crawford and Tony Lyons
(softcover, 6 × 9, 304 pages, $19.95)

Business and Legal Forms for Authors and Self-Publishers,
Revised Edition by Tad Crawford (softcover, 8½ × 11, 192 pages, $19.95)

Please write to request our free catalog. To order by credit card, call 1-800-491-2808 or send a check or money order to Allworth Press, 10 East 23rd Street, Suite 210, New York, NY 10010. Include $5 for shipping and handling for the first book ordered and $1 for each additional book. Ten dollars plus $1 for each additional book if ordering from Canada. New York State residents must add sales tax.

If you wish to see our complete catalog on the World Wide Web, you can find us at **www.allworth.com**

THE
TRADEMARK
GUIDE

by Lee Wilson

ALLWORTH PRESS
NEW YORK

Published by Allworth Press
An imprint of Allworth Communications
10 East 23rd Street, New York, NY 10010

Cover design by Douglas Designs, New York, NY

Book design by Sharp Des!gns, Lansing, MI

ISBN: 1-880559-81-1

Library of Congress Catalog Card Number: 97-72214

Printed in Canada

Dedication

This book is dedicated to my old friend and business partner Bill King, my favorite serial capitalist, whose accomplishments in the business world are proof that good ideas and hard work are rewarded in a free enterprise society.

————————————

Contents

Introduction

S MORE AND MORE of the wealth of our country becomes embodied in intellectual property, it becomes increasingly important for businesspeople to grasp the basics of intellectual-property law. Almost everyone has a hard time remembering the difference between the three major sorts of intellectual property: trademarks, copyrights, and patents. Trademarks are the subject of this book. Before you can completely understand trademarks, however, you need a passing knowledge of copyrights and patents. After we briefly distinguish trademarks from copyrights and patents, we'll consider trademarks in detail.

Although all three protect products of the human imagination, trademarks, copyrights, and patents are distinct but complementary types of intellectual property. Each is governed by a different federal law. The copyright and patent statutes both originate in Article I, Section 8, Clause 8 of the Constitution, which empowers Congress "to Promote the Progress of Science and useful Arts, by securing, for limited Times to Authors and Inventors, the exclusive Right to their respective Writings and Discoveries." Our federal trademark statute originates in the "commerce clause" of the Constitution, which gives Congress the power to regulate interstate commerce. Only our federal government regulates copyrights; copyright registrations are granted by the Copyright Office, which is a department of the Library of Congress. Similarly, only the federal government can grant a patent. However, although the federal government grants trademark registrations, so do all fifty states. And for complicated reasons, the U.S. Patent Office and the U.S. Trademark Office are two halves of the same division of the Department of Commerce, called the United States Patent and Trademark Office.

Confused? It gets easier. In fact, the best way to understand copyrights, patents, and trademarks is to consider them together, in relation to each other.

Copyrights

A copyright is a set of rights that the copyright statute gives to the creators of artistic, literary, musical, dramatic, and audiovisual works. Only the person who created the copyrighted work is legally permitted to reproduce, perform, or display it, distribute copies of it, or create variations of it; any unauthorized exercise of any of these rights is called "copyright infringement" and is actionable in federal court.

Since January 1, 1978, in the United States, a copyright is created whenever a creator "fixes" in tangible form a work for which copyright protection is available. Under most circumstances, a copyright will endure until fifty years after the death of the creator of the copyrighted work; after copyright protection expires, a work is said to have fallen into the "public domain" and anyone is free to use it. Registration of a copyright enhances the rights that a copyright owner gains automatically by the act of creation, but is not necessary for copyright protection. The chief limitation on the rights of copyright owners is that copyright protects only particular expressions of ideas rather than the ideas themselves. This means that several people can create copyrightable works based on the same idea; in fact, there is no infringement no matter how similar one work is to another unless one creator copied another's work.

(For more information about copyrights, see *The Copyright Guide,* published by Allworth Press.)

Patents

The word "patent" is used ordinarily to designate the rights granted by the federal government to the originator of a physical invention or industrial or technical process (a "utility patent") or an ornamental design for an "article of manufacture" (a "design patent"). A patent holder earns the exclusive right to make, use, and sell the invention, process, or design for which the patent was granted. Utility patents last seventeen years; design patents last fourteen years. Any unauthorized manufacture, use, or sale of the patented invention, process, or design within this country during the term of the patent is infringement.

(For more information about patents, see *The Patent Guide* by Carl Battle, also published by Allworth Press.)

Trademarks

Trademarks are words or designs that identify products or services to consumers. Unlike copyrights, in which their creators have protectable rights from the inception of the copyrighted work, rights in a trademark accrue only by use of the trademark in commerce and then belong to the company that applies the mark to its products rather than to the person who comes up with the name or designs the logo that becomes the trademark. Roughly speaking, a company gains rights in a trademark in proportion to the geographic scope and duration of its use of the mark; ordinarily, the company that uses a mark first gains rights in that mark superior to any other company that later uses it for the same product or services. Unauthorized use of a trademark is trademark infringement.

Trademark infringement is a commercial sin. It is one of the more common forms of a large and not-very-well-defined area of the law called "unfair competition." Basically, the law of unfair competition has, over the years and in numerous cases, labeled certain efforts at commercial competition "unfair"—even fraudulent—because they are too aggressive or less than honest. Unfair competition is, generally speaking, competition by dirty tricks, although several forms of unfair competition can result from otherwise innocent blunders. By declaring certain actions "unfair" in commerce, the courts seek to promote both free competition *and* fair competition. Among the types of trademark-related commercial conduct that have been held to constitute unfair competition are:

- trademark infringement,
- trademark dilution,
- use of confusingly similar business names,
- use of confusingly similar literary titles,
- the unauthorized use of a distinctive literary or performing style,
- copying a product's trade dress and configuration, and
- infringement of the right of publicity.

Not every action that has been or could be labeled unfair competition is codified, that is, enumerated and written down, in a statute. Judges may add to the list of unfair business tactics as new situations are presented that seem to them to entail overreaching by a marketer.

As is the case with copyrights, registration enhances rights in trademarks but does not create them. It is generally easy to register a mark within a state, but federal trademark registration, which confers much greater benefits, is more difficult to obtain. Trademark rights last indefinitely; as long as a mark is used in commerce, its owners have protectable rights in it.

A trademark represents the commercial reputation of a product or service as embodied in, usually, a word or design. Trademark law prohibits certain trade practices that are considered unfair, such as the imitation of another's trademark in order to profit from consumers' mistaken belief that the imitation trademark and the product it names are the real thing; this is trademark infringement. Trademark law also exists to protect consumers. It ensures, for instance, that when you buy a pair of running shoes marked with the NIKE® name, they are of the high quality you have come to expect in NIKE products because they are, indeed, manufactured by NIKE.

(Lawyers use capital letters to indicate the precise verbal content of trademarks; we'll do the same with all trademarks and with all titles, slogans, and names used like trademarks.)

The two things anyone who markets a product needs to know about trademarks are how to choose them and how to use them.

Choosing a new product name is not a simple undertaking, or should not be. Certain kinds of names are not registrable as trademarks with the U.S. Patent and Trademark Office; the knowledgeable businessperson who christens a new product will take these restrictions into account, since federal registration is, or should be, the goal of every trademark owner. The other major consideration in choosing a trademark is picking one that no one else is using. This process is called "trademark clearance." You ignore it at your peril, since adopting and using someone's established trademark, even innocently, is trademark infringement, and trademark infringement can result in lawsuits that are expensive to settle and hopelessly expensive to defend.

In the United States, trademark ownership accrues by use of the trademark in commerce. Unless a trademark is used in the marketplace, there is no trademark, because there is no commercial reputation that can be symbolized by the word or design. Roughly speaking, trademark owners earn the right to prevent others from using the same design or word to represent or name a product or service similar to theirs in direct proportion to the extent of their use of that name or design, geographically and otherwise.

The owner of the four Miss Miriam's ladies' clothing stores in northeast Idaho can probably keep other retailers from calling new clothing stores of any kind by the Miss Miriam's name or any name that is confusingly similar to Miss Miriam's only within the same general area—that is, within the geographic area where the commercial reputation of the stores has spread.

The long-standing fame of Bloomingdale's®, however, allows the company to stop the use of that or any confusingly similar name for a department or specialty clothing store anywhere in the United States, even in areas geographically remote from the famous New York store. Although the Bloomingdale's stores are physically located in and around New York City (and more recently Beverly

Hills), their reputation has spread across the United States and U.S. trademark law prohibits competitors anywhere in the country from competing with them unfairly by appropriating their famous name.

Once a trademark is "cleared for takeoff" and is in use, *how* the mark is used is very important. If a trademark is used as a noun rather than as an adjective ("WINKLES" rather than "WINKLES toy trucks"), it can lose its status as a trademark. That's what happened to "aspirin," "cellophane," and "escalator," all of which once named particular brands of the products for which they are now the generic names.

If the ® symbol is not used properly in conjunction with a federally registered trademark, the trademark owner's right to collect money damages in a lawsuit against a trademark infringer may be diminished.

In the abstract, these may seem like niggling considerations; in actuality, proper trademark usage can be crucial to the overall health of the company that owns the mark, since the company trademark may represent the most valuable asset of the company, its goodwill. The Xerox Company thinks so, at least. Otherwise it would not run thousands of dollars worth of ads every year pointing out that photocopiers are not "xerox machines" and that its machines are "XEROX® brand photocopiers."

Xerox doesn't want to end up like the Otis Elevator Company, whose famous ESCALATOR trademark ironically lost its uniqueness because of that very fame, thanks to the popularity and success of the moving stairways marketed under the ESCALATOR name. When the name ESCALATOR became a generic term applicable to all moving stairways, the ESCALATOR moving stairway was demoted to "escalator" and faded into the woodwork, so to speak, becoming so famous it became anonymous.

The chapters that follow contain the rest of the story. I hope I have told it well, because trademarks and the law and their interaction have consumed about a third of my working life. Like many English majors, after graduation from college I looked for areas of commerce where my love of language could be useful. I tried most of the usual ones: I have been a newspaper reporter; I wrote and produced advertising for several years; and I supported myself—

badly—during law school by working as a freelance writer. But I had missed one interesting area of the law that is especially suitable to anyone who cares about the effects of language (and symbols) on human behavior. Then, during my second and third years of law school, I clerked for a crusty but kind intellectual-property lawyer named Edwin Luedeka, who one day pointedly told me "trademark law is a good field for a woman." And for English majors, I found.

Trademark law is more like linguistics than any other area of the law. Once you grasp the real nature of trademarks, the intricacies of trademark law seem logical. And the importance of trademarks is hard to overstate, because nearly every dollar spent in our capitalistic society is directed into one corporate pocket rather than another because of the reputation of the product or service purchased, which is represented by its trademark.

This book is designed to be a primer for anyone who creates or uses trademarks, which is just about everyone employed in any management position in American business, whether that business is a one-person, headquarters-at-home, cottage industry or a giant corporation that employs thousands of people. Since I have nibbled at several of the edges of American business and have practiced trademark law for more than fifteen years, I believe I am well suited to talk about the issues, concerns, and problems of both trademark owners and of those who encounter trademarks in their business life and must know how to choose, handle, and protect them.

My twenty-year tutor in matters of business, especially start-up businesses, is my friend and business partner Bill King, to whom this book is dedicated. I am also indebted to another friend and lawyer, Larry Woods, for some of the ideas and insights in chapter 6; his years of experience helped me expand my own observations beyond the one-person-one-viewpoint barrier that faces anyone who writes on topics as broad as the legal profession.

I enjoy trademarks, although they sometimes make *my* head hurt. Trademarks are one variety of intangible creations of the human imagination that have a very tangible, dollars-and-cents effect on both our commercial and personal lives. I hope you find my fascination with trademarks informative and useful. If you live in America, chances are that you will play several innings in capitalism, a game even more characteristic of this country than either baseball or basketball. This book can help you avoid some of the pitfalls that can take out even talented players too early in the game.

Thanks, Mr. Luedeka.

♣

Understanding Trademarks

THIS IS A SHORT CHAPTER because, beyond knowing what a trademark is, as you must already know if you live in the United States, and how trademark ownership arises, which is not a very long story, the main thing you need to know about trademarks is how not to infringe them. We'll get to that just as soon as you really do understand trademarks.

The Lanham Act, which is a federal statute governing unfair competition and trademarks, defines a trademark as "any word, name, symbol or device or any combination thereof adopted and used by a manufacturer or merchant to identify his goods and distinguish them from those manufactured or sold by others." The statute defines a service mark as "a mark used in the sale or advertising of services to identify the services of one person and distinguish them from the services of others." A word or symbol qualifies as a trademark when it is both actually used in commerce to identify the goods or services of a manufacturer or merchant or provider of services and when it functions to identify and distinguish the goods or services from those of other manufacturers, merchants, or providers of services. More than one trademark may identify a product—think of the various logos and versions of the name used to market COCA-COLA® soft drinks.

In a free enterprise society, trademarks are everywhere. Trademarks are the guideposts of commerce; they embody the commercial reputations of products or services in the marketplace. Manufacturers use trademarks to communicate to consumers the origin of the products they market. Consumers use trademarks to help them find the particular products and services they want. Economists have declared that trademarks perform at least two market functions: (1) they encourage the production of quality products and (2) they make shopping easier by facilitating purchasing decisions. It seems clear that, as long as you can't thump a television set like a watermelon to decide whether to buy it, but must rely instead on what you know about the television manufacturer, trademarks will remain an important part of life in America.

We all rely on trademarks every day. Almost everything you use, from the coffee you drink to the mattress you sleep on, was bought by brand name, which is another way of saying "trademark." Nobody shows up with a checkbook at the nearest auto dealer and asks, simply, to buy "a car"; you drive a TOYOTA® or an INFINITI® or a VOLVO®, and you bought your car by name because of the reputation, for economy or prestige or reliability, that attaches to that car by its name. We avoid products we dislike, by name, and we seek out the ones we want, by name. These names come to mean something to the consumer; when you ask for CHANEL NO. 5® cologne at the perfume counter of a department store, you won't be satisfied by WHITE SHOULDERS® or OBSESSION®, and when you ask for a DIET COKE® at a fast-food drive-in window, you don't want DIET PEPSI®.

In the United States, a trademark owner gains rights in a particular name or logo for a product or service by using the name or the logo in the marketplace. ("Logos," short for "logotypes," are simply design trademarks, as opposed to names, which are verbal trademarks. Trademarks can also be combinations of names or words and designs or logos. Service marks are the variety of trademarks that name services. For simplicity's sake, the general term "trademark" or simply "mark," will be used here to refer to both the names or symbols for services and those for products.)

It is very important to understand that in this country trademark rights are gained by use of a mark, not by registration of it. State or federal registration of a trademark enhances the rights of the owner of the trademark and serves as notice to others of ownership of the mark, but a business that uses a trademark in the marketplace owns the right to use that mark *because* of that use—unless some other business has a better claim to it through longer and/or wider use—whether or not the mark is ever registered. Trademark ownership is also determined by *priority* of use: to own a trademark, you must do more than simply use it in the marketplace, you must also be the *first* to use the mark. In other words, a person or company acquires rights in a trademark roughly commensurate with the length of use, the geographic scope of use, and the variety of commercial uses it makes of the mark. That is, a large company that has long marketed a variety of products across the U.S. under its trademark has a much stronger claim to its mark and is much better able to halt anyone else's use of any similar mark for any similar products than does a recently established mom-and-pop company that sells its products only in the city where it is located.

Nor can registration perpetuate the existence of a moribund trademark. If a trademark owner ceases for too long to use a trademark in the marketplace, that owner can lose all ownership rights in the mark, regardless of whether the mark has been registered. Without *use* of a name to market a product or service, there *is* no trademark—the name has ceased to embody a current reputation for the product or service to which it was applied. Think of it this way: a person's reputation dies with him or her—that is, the reputation that remains after someone's death is only the memory of that person's actions in life. Because a person's activities cease at death, his or her reputation does not continue to accrue in the present. The same is true of trademarks, which are simply the reputations of products and services. If there is no use of a trademark in the channels of commerce, the reputation of the product or service formerly marketed under that trademark becomes defunct.

Anyone who is involved in the marketing process knows what enormous effort and expense go into developing and publicizing new products. Trademark law allows companies that spend time and money developing their market shares to reap the benefits of that effort. Trademark law lets you enjoy the benefits of your own commercial reputation and prohibits anyone else from taking a free ride on your commercial coattails. It also protects consumers by allowing them to spend their money on the products and services they have grown to trust.

Almost anything can be a trademark so long as it is used on a product or in advertising a service in such a manner as to indicate the origin of the product or service. In other words, trademarks answer two questions: *who made the product* and *who renders the service*. All the following can and do serve as trademarks because consumers have come to associate them with the products and services they are used to market.

- words (ACE® bandages, PLEDGE® furniture polish)
- names (WATERMAN® fountain pens, HARTMANN® luggage)
- designs (the embroidered JORDACHE® jeans hip pocket design, the famous Coca-Cola "dynamic ribbon device")
- slogans ("WHEN IT RAINS, IT POURS®")
- drawings (Prudential's Rock of Gibraltar logo)
- likenesses of fictitious people (BETTY CROCKER®, the Quaker Oats Quaker man)
- likenesses of living people (Paul Newman's image used as a logo for NEWMAN'S OWN® salad dressing)
- likenesses of deceased people (Colonel Harlan Sanders's image on KENTUCKY FRIED CHICKEN® containers)
- literary characters (all the main characters in the Star Wars movies are also trademarks for a variety of goods)
- abbreviations and nicknames (BUD® for BUDWEISER® beer, VW® for VOLKSWAGEN® automobiles, HOG® for large HARLEY-DAVIDSON® motorcycles)
- initials (IBM®, CBS®, A&W®)
- radio and television station call letters and radio broadcast frequency designations (WSM® radio, WTBS® television, WGBH® television; RADIO 1430)
- telephone numbers (DIAL-A-MATTRESS® for home mattress delivery)
- numbers (A-1® steak sauce, V8® vegetable juice)

- music or songs (the SESAME STREET® television show theme song)
- package designs (the well-known CHANEL NO. 5® perfume bottle shape)
- architectural features of businesses (the McDONALD'S® hamburger restaurants' golden arches)

In most cases, common geometric shapes and colors do not function as trademarks until they have acquired "secondary meaning," which means that a mark used to market a product or service has become famous enough to be associated with one particular marketer.

Businesspeople often encounter trademarks in what is perhaps the most critical period of their existence—their birth. When this happens, they are being asked to "incubate" brand-new trademarks. Designing a new corporate logo or design trademark is one of the most important business functions you will undertake. Naming a product well is nearly as challenging as naming a new baby. (Either task is also risky, perhaps more so than any other creative activity undertaken for a business purpose.) That's because we are running out of trademarks. That is, we have more trademarks than ever before bombarding us, seeking to attract our attention in magazine and television and billboard ads. What we are running out of is material for new trademarks; we are approaching the almost unbelievable number of 100,000 registrations for *new* trademarks *each year* in the U.S. Trademark Office. This is *in addition to* the nearly 1 million currently valid United States trademarks already registered. With such a deluge of new trademarks annually joining the existing vast reservoir of active marks, it is easy to understand why it has become very difficult to avoid infringing an existing trademark when you design a new logo or name a new product. It can be done, however, and the next chapter will tell you how.

❖

Trademark Infringement 101

A TRADEMARK REPRESENTS the commercial reputation of a product or service in the marketplace. Trademark owners often expend enormous amounts of money in establishing and promoting their trademarks. Once established, a trademark may be one of the most valuable assets owned by a company. (Think of the Coca-Cola Company; its various COCA-COLA® and COKE® trademarks are worth far more than the physical assets of the company.) Consequently, trademark owners act quickly against anyone who encroaches upon their trademarks. Adopting the wrong trademark can land you in a lawsuit for trademark infringement, even if you had no knowledge when you chose your trademark that it might infringe another trademark. This means that care in choosing a name for a new product or service is very important. Unfortunately, trademark selection in this country is, for the uninformed, a little like Russian roulette.

Imagine this scenario. After you've made three separate presentations and long after you've given up hope of landing the account, someone from the marketing department of the Omega Corporation calls to say that they have chosen your ad agency to handle all their U.S. advertising. Seems they were impressed with your proposals and have decided to give their business to an agency in your city, where they have their home office. They are happy with their decision. You are happy with their decision. You and your partners hire two more artists and a new copywriter and get to work on your first big Omega assignment, developing an ad campaign to break their new product, a universal television/VCR remote control that will work with all Omega Electronics products and with those of most other manufacturers as well.

But before you can advertise the new remote, you have to name it, so you and your three best creative people retire to your conference room late one afternoon to think of the perfect name. After several loud arguments, two six-packs, and more than three hours of intense brainstorming, you reach a consensus.

You and your staff like the name UNI-TROL. So do the Omega marketing people, when you present the name to them. They give you the go-ahead on the whole project and, simultaneously, a tight deadline. They want to have their product in the stores before the beginning of the new fall television season, and they authorize you to do whatever is necessary to complete on time all the packaging and advertising materials they need. You roll up your shirtsleeves, work a lot of late nights, and meet their deadlines.

The new product is a hit. There is no other product like it that is as inexpensive or as simple to operate. Sales are through the roof. You starting thinking of buying a new car. Then, out of the blue, you get an outraged call from the head of the Omega marketing department. He's just learned that the Omega Corporation has been sued in federal court for trademark infringement by a big New York law firm representing a German corporation that owns U.S. and Canadian trademark registrations it says are infringed by the name you created.

It seems that the German corporation, Unicorp, markets various sorts of electronic equipment around the world under various trademarks, all of which begin with UNI-. They are asking the court for an award of money damages and the profits from Omega's marketing of the UNI-TROL remote, plus an injunction that would force Omega to recall all its remotes previously distributed under the Uni-Trol name, to destroy all packaging and advertising materials that use or bear the offending name, and to cease using, immediately and forever, the trademark by which the public knows the new product, Uni-Trol. There is no joy in Mudville.

The only people who are not unhappy about the trademark-infringement lawsuit are the lawyers hired by the Omega Corporation to defend it. They know that some of the money you thought Omega would spend with your agency is now going to be consumed by their legal fees.

The saddest news of all is hearing that Omega's lawyers have said that Omega's use of the Uni-Trol mark does infringe the Unicorp marks and that, under the circumstances, the best thing for Omega to do is to cut its losses and immediately pull all the Uni-Trol television and print ads and stop distributing the remotes completely until a new name and new packaging and promotional materials can be developed. Which, of course, means that what Omega's dealers will remember about Omega's innovative remote control product is that (1) somebody goofed in naming it and (2) that goof destroyed the momentum the product initially gained in the market, cutting their profits. And what Omega will remember, regrettably, is that you proposed the name that is causing all the trouble.

None of this had to happen. In almost every case, trademark-infringement problems can be avoided by the proper attention at the right time to a few simple considerations.

Had you been better informed, you would have made some effort to check on the availability of the Uni-Trol mark when you proposed it to Omega, by recommending to Omega that it have a trademark search conducted or by commissioning one yourself, on behalf of Omega.

A "full" trademark search, that is, a search of United States federal and state registrations as well as of data regarding valid but unregistered marks, would have turned up the "family" of Uni-marks owned by Unicorp and registered in the United States for various electronic products. The lawyer interpreting the trademark search report would have picked up the phone and called you and recommended that you go back to the drawing board for the new Omega mark. The whole process would have taken no more than ten business days and cost about $600 or $700, lawyer's fees included; an expedited search could have been performed, for an increased fee, in as little as twenty-four hours.

You could have chosen another good name for the remote. Omega could have liked it. The lawsuit might still be in the back pocket of the Unicorp lawyers. And all those carefully produced UNI-TROL ads and materials could be winning you awards instead of gathering dust in an Omega warehouse somewhere.

But perfect hindsight is poor consolation. What you really need is to know enough about trademark infringement to avoid it. Lots of trademark disputes arise because trademarks are chosen solely on the basis of artistic merit and the image they will create in the advertising media. Those are, of course, important considerations; coming up with a name that fits the new product and will attract consumers is a hard thing to do. However, the other hard part of naming a new product or service is finding a name that doesn't infringe an established mark. That part of the process can make you wish you'd gone to dental school.

Trademark infringement usually results because someone has chosen for a new product or service a name that is the same as or is very similar to a mark that has been used longer for the same or a similar or related product or service. In the United States, trade-mark ownership is created by use of a mark; generally speaking, the first company to begin using a mark owns it. Once a company has established ownership of a mark, anyone else who uses the mark for a similar product or service is said to be "infringing" the rights of the trademark owner. This means that any proposed trademark must be evaluated to determine whether it will infringe an estab-lished mark.

The test courts apply in determining infringing similarity between marks is "likelihood of confusion"; that is, are consumers likely to confuse the new name with the older, established trademark because of the similarity of the marks? The similarity between marks is gauged by what is called the "sight, sound, and meaning test." This means that you want to avoid choosing for a new mark any word and/or design that looks so much like and sounds so much like and has a meaning so like an established trademark that represents a similar product that consumers will mistake the new mark for the established mark. The degree of resemblance between conflicting marks is analyzed by a comparison of the following characteristics of the marks: (1) the overall impressions created by the marks, (2) the pronunciations of the marks, (3) the translations of foreign words that are elements of the marks, (4) the verbal translations of visual elements of the marks, and (5) the suggestions, connotations, or meanings of the marks. If there are enough similarities between the marks that it is probable that the average buyer will confuse the products or services the marks represent, or believe that the new product or service is somehow related to the owner of the older mark, the new mark infringes the older mark. Confusing similarity does not exist when it is merely *possible* that consumers will confuse the similar marks, but, rather, when such confusion is *probable.*

Generally, infringement occurs only when similar or identical marks name similar or related products or services. However, this is not always true in the case of "strong" trademarks. Strong marks, because they have achieved broad reputations, enjoy broad protection from upstart imitators who try to capitalize on their fame and distinctiveness by associating themselves with the famous marks. KODAK®, COCA-COLA®, and LEVI'S® are examples of strong verbal marks; the "woolmark" design logo of the International Wool Secretariat, the "Morton Salt girl" character trademark, and the Shell Oil Company logo are examples of strong trademarks that consist largely or only of design or visual elements. It is a very good idea to give famous trademarks a wide berth when naming any product or service, even if the new product or service is very different from those named by the famous marks, since most owners of widely advertised and well-known marks protect their trademarks vigorously.

All this sounds a lot harder than it usually is. Since "confusing similarity" is evaluated as if through the eyes and/or ears of an average consumer, you can function as your own first line of defense against choosing a trademark that infringes another trademark. In other words, if you think your new mark might infringe an older mark, you're probably right.

Keep in mind that it is not necessary that a new mark be *identical* to an established mark in order to infringe it. In fact, the degree of similarity necessary to constitute infringement varies depending on the similarity between the two products or services named by the marks. When the products or services are directly competitive, less similarity will constitute infringement; when they are not directly competitive and/or are sold in different channels of trade, more similarity is necessary to constitute infringement. A few examples will give you a feel for the degree of similarity between trademarks that constitutes "confusing similarity."

BEARCAT for trucks will infringe BEARCAT for boats or tires or travel trailers, but not for, say, bicycles or hunting boots or police scanner radios.

TWINKLE TOYS for a child's building block set will infringe the famous TINKER TOYS® trademark. Call your new block set TWINKLE BLOCKS, though, and you're probably safe.

ZESTA® for saltines does not infringe SHASTA® for soft drinks. Calling any food item the same name as any other food item, however, is asking for a lawsuit, no matter how different the two varieties of food. The reasoning behind this rule is that consumers can reasonably assume that a manufacturer of one food item has begun marketing another under the same trademark.

This sort of association confusion as to the origin of a product is a variety of trademark infringement. For example, the manufacturer of GOLD MEDAL® flour might not like having its commercial reputation confused by being mistakenly believed to be the maker of GOLD MEDAL ice cream, even if the ice cream is very good ice cream.

Bear in mind that the categories of products or services named by the marks are very important in making any evaluation of possible infringement. A breakfast roll named BON JOUR probably won't infringe the mark of a department store named BON JOUR, because rolls are far removed from department store services, both in their consumers and in the channels of trade in which they are offered.

However, as we have seen, strong marks transcend the boundaries between categories of products and services. BON JOUR for a brand of breakfast rolls could infringe the trademark rights of the owners of a famous restaurant named BON JOUR, for a combination of the reasons just mentioned; that is, because consumers, familiar with the reputation of the famous restaurant, might believe that breakfast rolls were a new product of the restaurant.

Generally, infringement results when the inherent similarity between two marks is "multiplied" by the degree of similarity of the products or services the marks name and the fame of the established mark. At some point, these factors reach a critical mass and ignite into a trademark-infringement lawsuit.

In the case of logos or design marks that have no verbal content, the standard for judging confusing similarity is the same as that used to evaluate the similarity between word trademarks, with the exception, of course, that a mark without any words has no "sound when spoken." With logos or design marks, you must carefully compare the appearance of the proposed logo or design mark with that of all other marks that designate similar products or services, including marks that are combinations of words and design elements. You must also consider the implications of the design elements of your proposed mark; that is, will your star logo infringe an existing mark for a similar product named STAR?

Judging similarity between logos or the design elements of marks is often more difficult than judging similarity between verbal marks because the similarity between visual elements may be much more subtle.

It is hard to talk about design trademarks in print, but a few examples of confusion between design trademarks are possible.

Any white-on-red or red-on-white curve at all similar to the famous Coca-Cola double-curve design trademark used for any soft drink will infringe Coke's famous trademark. However, a similar curve in another color combination used for, say, a brand of farm equipment, might escape challenge.

Similarly, any design of any deer or deer-like animal used for insurance services or related services, such as financial services, would probably infringe the famous hundred-plus-year-old Hartford Insurance Company standing-stag design trademark. Use your deer for ice cream, however, and you are safe.

Any clown design or character used to advertise a fast-food restaurant, whether like McDonald's Ronald McDonald trademark character or not, would probably be viewed by McDonald's as infringing upon its famous clown trademark. If your clown design or character was very different from our friend Ronald (perhaps a female clown named Pandora who wears a yellow wig and dresses all in pink), you could safely use her picture and an actress dressed like her to advertise and promote children's shoes.

Employ any depiction of a tipped cup perpetually losing the "last drop" of coffee and you will run afoul of Maxwell House. You may even get into trouble by using such a depiction in signage for a chain of coffee shops, since consumers could reasonably believe that the shops serve or otherwise have some association with MAXWELL HOUSE® coffee. Set your coffee cup upright on its saucer, however, and it is probably safe to use for coffee shops.

The famous Columbia Broadcasting System "eye" symbol is as effective today as it was when first designed in 1958. That means that any abstract or realistic eye design used for any product or service that is even remotely connected with broadcasting or television or film production is going to be challenged by CBS. You can use a dissimilar, realistic depiction of the human eye as the logo for franchise optometry shops, however, without looking over your shoulder to see if CBS is watching.

Ignore these analyses at your peril. Owners of established marks are quick to send cease and desist letters to marketers of new products who tread on their marks. An example of a cease and desist letter is reproduced in the appendix of this book. Names have been faked to protect the guilty, but this is essentially the text of an actual letter sent in circumstances very similar to those mentioned.

Too Close for Comfort

The following pairs of trademarks were held by courts to be confusingly similar when used in conjunction with identical or similar products.

AMERIBANC and BANK OF AMERICA
ARISE and AWAKE
ARM & HAMMER and ARM IN ARM
ARROW and AIR-O
AVEDA and AVITA
BEAUTY-REST and BEAUTY SLEEP
BECK'S BEER and EX BIER
BEEP and VEEP

BLOCKBUSTER VIDEO and VIDEO BUSTER

BLUE NUN and BLUE ANGEL

BLUE SHIELD and RED SHIELD

BLUE THUNDER and BLUE LIGHTNING

BREW MISER and COFFEE MISER

BUST RUST and RUST BUSTER

CAESARS PALACE and TRUMP'S PALACE

CAT TRAC and KATRACK

CENTURY 21 and CENTURY 31

CHAT NOIR and BLACK CAT (foreign language equivalent meanings can constitute infringing similarity)

CITIBANK and CITY BANK

CITY GIRL and CITY WOMAN

COCA-COLA and CLEO COLA

COMSAT and COMCET

CRISTÓBAL COLON and CHRISTOPHER COLUMBUS

CYCLONE and TORNADO

DAN RIVER, DAN MASTER, DAN TWILL, DAN TONE, DAN and DANFRA (a new mark that is even somewhat similar to an established family of marks can infringe those related marks by being mistakenly believed to be merely a new addition to the "family")

DATSUN and DOTSON

DELL and BELL

DERNIER TOUCHE and THE FINAL TOUCH

DOWNTOWNER and UPTOWNER

DRAMAMINE and BONAMINE

EL GALLO and THE ROOSTER

EST EST EST and IT IS IT IS IT IS

FACE TO FACE and CHEEK TO CHEEK

FIRM 'N GENTLE and NICE 'N GENTLE

GASTOWN and GAS CITY

GENTLE TOUCH and KIND TOUCH

GOOD MORNING and BUENOS DÍAS

HERITAGE and HERMITAGE

HINT O'HONEY and HIDDEN HONEY

JOUJOU and JOJO

KAHLÚA and CHULA

KEY and a picture trademark in the form of a representation of a key

KNORR and NOR-KING
LISTERINE and LISTOGEN
LONDON FOG and SMOG
LORRAINE and LA TOURAINE
MANPOWER and WOMENPOWER
MEDI-ALERT and MEDIC ALERT
MENNEN and MINON
MIRACLE WHIP and SALAD WHIP
MOUNTAIN KING and ALPINE KING
NIKON and IKON
OLD FORESTER and OLD FOSTER
ORKIN and ORKO
PHILADELPHIA and PENNSYLVANIA
PIZZERIA UNO and TACO UNO
PLAY-DOH and FUN DOUGH
PLEDGE and PROMISE
PORSCHE and PORSHA
RAIN BARREL and RAIN FRESH
ROCKLAND MORTGAGE CORP. and ROCKWELL NATIONAL
     MORTGAGE
SAVINGS SHOP and THE SAVINGS SPOT
SEIKO and SEYCOS
SILVER FLASH and SUPER FLASH
SMIRNOFF and SARNOFF
SNAPPY and SNIPPY
S.O. and ESSO
SPARKLETTS and SPRINKLETS
SQUIRT and QUIRST
STEINWAY and STEINWEG
TELECHRON and TELICON
TORO ROJO and RED BULL
TOYS "R" US and KIDS "R" US
TRAK and TRAQ
ULTRA BRITE and ULTRA-DENT
ULTRA VELVET and ULTRA SUEDE
WEED EATER and LEAF EATER
YAMAHA and MAKAHA

Close, but No Cigar

Think you've got the hang of it? Maybe not. The following pairs of trademarks were held by courts *not* to be confusingly similar when used in conjunction with identical or similar products.

ACCUTRON and UNITRON

AFTER TAN and APRÉS SUN

BANK IN A BILLFOLD and BANK IN A WALLET

BOSTON TEA PARTY and BOSTON SEA PARTY

CAR-X and EXXON

COCA-COLA and COCO LOCO

COCA-COLA and THE UNCOLA

CREAM OF WHEAT and CREAMY WHEAT

DAWN and DAYLIGHT

DUVET and DUET

FILM FUN and MOVIE HUMOR

FRUIT OF THE LOOM and FRUIT OF THE EARTH

GREEN LEAF and BLACK LEAF (when applied to plant sprays, the marks
    have opposite meanings)

HELICARB and HELI COIL

HOUR AFTER HOUR and SHOWER TO SHOWER

100 YEAR NITE-LITE and CENTURY NIGHT LIGHT

L'AIR DU TEMPS and L'AIR D'OR

LONG JOHN and FRIAR JOHN

MARSHALL FIELD'S and MRS. FIELDS

MATCH and MACHO

MOTHER BESSIE'S and MOTHER'S BEST

MR. CLEAN and MASTER KLEEN

PECAN SANDIES and PECAN SHORTEES

REJUVA-NAIL and REJUVIA

SATIN QUICK and SUDDENLY SATIN

SILKY TOUCH and TOUCH O'SILK

SUBARU and SUPRA

SURF and SURGE

TIC TAC TOE and TIC TAC

T.G.I. FRIDAY'S and E.L. SATURDAY'S

TACO TOWN and TACO TIME

THUNDERBOLT and THUNDERBIRD
TORNADO and TYPHOON
VANTAGE and ADVANCE
WHEATIES and OATIES
WINTERIZER and WINTERSTAT

Is It Infringement?

Q. You have been famous for years among your friends and relatives for your plum preserves and decide to market them. You tell the graphic designer you hire to create the label for your preserves that you really like the red-and-white "gingham" labels for the popular MABEL'S line of jellies and jams and you want to use something similar for your own labels. You love the label he designs; it is identical to the MABEL'S labels except that instead of "MABEL'S," it says "NATALIE'S," and there is a little sketch of a basket of ripe plums where the MABEL'S labels use drawings of various fruits on the vine. You show your design to the lawyer who is helping you meet FDA labeling requirements for your preserves. He frowns when he sees it and tells you that you need to go back to the drawing board, since he believes the Mabel's Company will have grounds for suit if you use your label as it is. You don't see why he thinks there is a problem; NATALIE'S certainly doesn't sound like MABEL'S, or look like it, or have the same meaning. And you are marketing *plum* preserves—the Mabel's Company markets strawberry, blackberry, peach, and grape jams and jellies, but *no* plum preserves, and it has never used a drawing of a basket of plums on its labels. The question is: *Is it infringement?*

A. Sorry, but your lawyer is right. Insofar as it goes, your information as to what constitutes trademark infringement is correct, but, as the saying goes, a little knowledge is a dangerous thing. In isolation, NATALIE'S for preserves does not infringe MABEL'S for jams and jellies because it doesn't sound sufficiently like MABEL'S, or look enough like it, or have a similar enough meaning, to be likely to confuse consumers. However, you are overlooking an important factor in the analysis of possible infringement—"overall commercial impression." If you think about it, you will have to admit that the overall commercial impression created by your label design would be extremely similar to that created by the MABEL'S labels. Consumers could easily confuse your product with MABEL'S products because the small differences in their labels would not be apparent to a busy shopper who reaches for a familiar red-and-white "gingham" label, especially since your product and the MABEL'S products would be shelved in the same section of grocery stores and both use a woman's given name as a trademark.

If you proceed with your plan to use the red-and-white knockoff label, MABEL'S will sue you for trade dress infringement as well as for trademark infringement, as soon as it notices your products. Trade dress infringement is related to trademark infringement. It is the unauthorized adoption of another marketer's packaging design, colors, typeface, and even container shape. It is presumed to be an effort to pass off the copycat product as the more established product by the use of the established product's characteristic commercial "costume."

Your dilemma is not quite the situation that exists when the names of two vastly different kinds of food products are similar. There is a long-established rule that a name for *any* food product will infringe the same or a very similar name for any other food product. As we have seen, this is because the original user of the name could easily be presumed to have expanded its line to include the new food product named by the similar name. After all, no one would be surprised if General Mills added, say, frozen prepared cakes to its line of BETTY CROCKER® cake mixes. Here, you must take into consideration more than the name of your product, since consumers recognize products by more than just their names.

Ask your designer to create a label with a solid plum-colored background—no gingham checks—and your preserves will get you into stores and keep you out of court.

Q. You name your fledgling messenger service FLASH MESSENGER SERVICE and embroider a gold lightning bolt on the caps and shirts your messengers wear and paint it on the sides of your delivery vans. You are very happy with your creativity until you receive a call from the owner of another local messenger service, LIGHTNING MESSENGER SERVICE. It seems that for twenty years LIGHTNING

MESSENGER SERVICE has used a lightning bolt design as its logo. The owner of the Lightning Company is very unhappy that his only competitor in town has adopted what he thinks is his sole property in what he insinuates is a transparent effort to trade on Lightning's good reputation. You tell him you will get back to him and call your cousin Megan, who is a third-year law student. You ask Megan: *Is it infringement?*

A. If Megan was in class the day her intellectual-property law professor talked about trademark infringement, she will answer, immediately and unambiguously, "Yes." One of the factors considered in comparing two marks for the possibility of conflict is the meaning of visual elements of the marks. Here, your lightning bolt logo infringes the trademark rights of the owner of LIGHTNING MESSENGER SERVICE in two ways. First, your use of the same symbol for your logo as that long used by Lightning is likely to confuse consumers. Secondly, the reasonable verbal meaning of your logo is "lightning." This will certainly add to the likelihood that consumers will confuse the two messenger services. The best course for you may be to immediately retire your lightning bolt caps and shirts and repaint your vans to eliminate the infringing symbol that is on its way to getting you named as a defendant in a trademark-infringement suit you are likely to lose. You'll at least save yourself the considerable costs of defending a suit that is a losing proposition. And maybe you can pay Megan for her help by shipping her a dozen or so slightly used lightning bolt shirts. She could probably use them; law students never get around to doing laundry.

Q. The day after you celebrate the first anniversary of your popular coffee shop, CAFÉ AU LAIT, you get a strange call from someone trying to make dinner reservations who seems to think that you serve Spanish food. Two days later, you get another such call. You decide that the moon must be full and think no more about the calls until you notice a new restaurant that has just opened near your favorite shopping center. The restaurant is called CAFÉ OLÉ and, upon investigation, you discover that it serves Spanish food. You are worried. If people calling information for the CAFÉ OLÉ phone number are being given your number, what is happening to *your* calls—and customers? You call CAFÉ OLÉ and express your concerns to the manager. He dismisses your concerns and tells you that your coffee shop and his Spanish restaurant are not in competition for customers and that, even if the names of your respective establishments sound alike when spoken, they don't look alike in print and don't have similar meanings. You are unconvinced and remain worried. You hang up and call your lawyer. You want to ask: *Is it infringement?*

A. Your lawyer will confirm your suspicions that your predicament is a case of trademark infringement. Regardless of the difference between CAFÉ AU LAIT and CAFÉ OLÉ, the fact that their pronunciations are indistinguishable to the average ear is already resulting in what is called in trademark law "actual confusion"—in this case, the misdirection by telephone information operators of consumers who want CAFÉ OLÉ to your coffee shop and, possibly, vice versa. When proven in court, this is prima facie evidence of trademark infringement; in other words, proving that the likelihood of confusion between two marks is no longer merely a likelihood, but has become a continuing reality, is sufficient to convince any judge in a trademark-infringement lawsuit that the plaintiff's rights are being infringed. Lucky for you that you applied for and were granted a federal registration for CAFÉ AU LAIT, since federal registration is a prerequisite for bringing a trademark-infringement lawsuit in federal court and can affect the damages the judge will award you and greatly diminish the costs you will incur to press your case.

Q. You and another freshly minted M.B.A. take the plunge and open your own computer components business. You choose as your logo a sphere divided into stripes in the colors of the visible spectrum (violet, blue, green, yellow, orange, and red), in order. The name of your products is SPECTRUM; that name and your striped-sphere logo appear on your stationery, on every one of your products, on all packaging materials, and in your ads. You have just ordered the production of 10,000 of your popular trackballs to fill your biggest order yet when you get a cease and desist letter from lawyers for Macintosh, who are insistent that your logo infringes the famous Macintosh striped-apple-with-a-bite-out-of-it logo. You are indignant. You think that the Macintosh lawyers are just bullies who want to put a competitor out of business. You do not believe your logo infringes the Macintosh trademark; your logo is a sphere, not an apple, and your stripes are the colors of the spectrum, in order, while the Apple logo uses those colors in another combination (green, yellow, orange, red, violet, and blue). And you know that SPECTRUM doesn't look or sound anything like MACINTOSH® or APPLE®, nor does it have a meaning similar to either mark. You put in a call to the lawyer who handles your patent filings to find out if you can simply ditch the letter from Macintosh. What you want to ask him is: *Is it infringement?*

A. Unfortunately, your lawyer is going to tell you that you can't ignore Macintosh's letter because you are, indeed, treading on their trademark. Then he will tell you why. His explanation will sound something like this: the minor differences you can point to between your striped-sphere logo and Macintosh's striped-apple logo are immaterial. In a comparison of marks for infringement, the overall commercial impression created by the marks is determinative. In a proper analysis, the marks are not dissected and their minor dissimilarities tallied and totaled; rather, the total effect they have on consumers who encounter them in their "natural habitats," i.e., in the environments where they are sold, is judged. This impression is created in a matter of seconds in most settings where consumers encounter trademarks, and it is created primarily by the dominant elements of the trademarks. *Any* element of a trademark can be the dominant element because dominance can be produced by almost any characteristic of any element of a trademark: the uniqueness of the element, its size relative to other elements of the mark, its color, its visual appeal, its memorability, etc. Your striped-sphere and Macintosh's striped-apple logo are more dominant than the verbal marks used with them (SPECTRUM and MACINTOSH®, respectively) because they are more colorful and more visually appealing.

Consumers are not likely to pause in electronics stores to note that the colored stripes in your logo are the colors of the visible spectrum, in order, as opposed to the same colors in different order in the Macintosh logo, which is an apple, as opposed to your sphere. They may, however, decide that since your products bear what they may mistake for the Macintosh logo, the Spectrum name refers merely to a new line of Macintosh products. This is, of course, infringement.

Further, products like computer components are marketed worldwide. The visual elements of a trademark are even more important in international commerce since consumers who can't understand or remember an English verbal trademark will have no such difficulty with a memorable visual mark. It is even more likely that consumers outside the U.S. will confuse your logo with the Macintosh apple.

The last thing your lawyer says is that you could have avoided this problem—and the expense of discarding and redesigning everything that bears your old logo, including your stationery, your current ad campaign, and most of a small warehouse full of packaging materials, not to mention figuring out how to stick new logos over the infringing ones on the housings for several thousand computer components—by the simple expedient of a trademark-design search to clear your logo for use. Your protestations that you *did* clear Spectrum are of no avail. In reality, the name of your products, Spectrum, and your logo are two separate trademarks, usually used together, but distinct and equally capable of infringing another mark. Real life business teaches harder lessons than business school.

Q. You and your buddies have formed what you think is the next big rock band to emerge from an American garage. You know that trademarks are important in marketing bands, so you put some time into coming up with a name. The name you choose, Kinxs (pronounced "kinks"), suits everybody but your drummer, a second-year law student who thinks he knows everything. He likes the name but says that you will be hauled into federal court by the famous band INXS® (pronounced "in excess") for trademark infringement if you use it. You don't believe him because you don't think the names are similar enough to cause a problem and, anyway, despite your delusions of rock-and-roll grandeur, you know that your band is obscure and not likely to be famous enough for some time to attract the attention of the lawyers for any other act. Should you listen to your know-it-all drummer? Or, in other words: *Is it infringement?*

A. Sorry, Charlie. KINXS and INXS® *are* pronounced differently, at least by those familiar with rock bands, and have very different meanings, but their appearance in print, in ads, and on album covers is very similar. INXS is an unusual name and the band that owns it is famous; it is very dangerous to get too close to unusual trademarks that name famous products or services because the "name recognition" of such marks is so high that people are more likely to mistake similar marks for the famous ones. Further, marks that are similar to famous marks are likely to run up against the proscriptions of the Trademark Dilution Act, which will only furnish the lawyers for INXS with further ammunition. (See chapter 5 for more detailed information about the Trademark Dilution Act.) And your complacent attitude that your band is too obscure ever to come to the attention of those lawyers is only justified to a point, because obscurity will work as a shield only so long. What usually happens with any trademark accused of infringing a more famous mark is that the upstart mark will come to the attention of the owners of the famous mark at about the time it is beginning to gain some fame. This is bad news for the owners of the new mark, because it means a lawsuit that could result in the necessity to abandon the new mark at just the point when it is becoming well-known enough to result in some money. It is always better to adopt a new trademark that you can sink your hard work into without fear that you may be compelled to abandon it.

❖

CHAPTER 3

Trademark Clearance

THE FIRST STEP in avoiding infringing an established trademark is to consciously avoid choosing for your new product or service a name or design that is identical or closely similar to another trademark that is already in use for a similar or related product or service.

This seems too obvious to mention, but it needs to be said. More than a few trademark-infringement lawsuits have been filed because someone mistakenly thought that because a name or design worked once it could work again. This means that in developing ideas for a new trademark, you should ask anybody who proposes one where the idea came from. Ignorance of trademark law will not save you from a trademark-infringement lawsuit if you step on the toes of a trademark owner determined to protect its established mark.

And it doesn't matter that you came up with the proposed new trademark without the knowledge of the established mark that it infringes; if it infringes the older mark, the source of your proposed mark is irrelevant. Nor will changing a few letters or design elements in an existing mark or spelling it differently or even combining it with other words or symbols save you from a charge of infringement, unless the changes you make are so significant that they eradicate the confusing similarity between the old and new marks.

The second important way to avoid trademark disputes is the trademark search, which is a search made by a professional trademark search firm to locate any established trademarks that are similar enough to your proposed mark to be confused with it. The trademark search firm will examine federal and state trademark registration records and data on unregistered but currently used marks and will compile data on marks similar to the proposed mark in a trademark search report.

Because this data needs interpretation, which is not furnished by the trademark search firm, you really need a lawyer for a trademark search, contrary to what you will hear occasionally from even reputable trademark search firms. A lawyer will properly instruct the search firm as to the direction and scope of the search when commissioning it, will evaluate the raw data in the search report, and will give a legal opinion assessing the degree of risk, if any, involved if the proposed mark is adopted.

And not just any lawyer will do. You need a *trademark lawyer* to conduct a trademark search after you have narrowed your proposed marks to two or three possibilities. There is a detailed discussion of how to find a trademark lawyer and what to do with him or her when you find one in chapter 6.

Be prepared to find out that your favorite proposed mark is already being used by someone else; it happens every day to some designer or advertising creative person who spent weeks developing what she or he believed to be a unique new mark. The good news is that it is much easier and much less expensive to discard a proposed mark before any money is spent advertising it than to abandon a new trademark six months into your first big promotion of it.

Pages from two hypothetical trademark search reports conducted to clear the name for a hamburger restaurant, along with the opinion letters written by the lawyer who evaluated the searches, are reproduced in the appendix. (Real trademark search reports are often forty to fifty pages long; the only pages reproduced from these hypothetical reports are the search summary pages, which list briefly only the federally registered trademarks located by the search.)

These search reports and opinion letters illustrate the process of elimination that occurs during trademark clearance. YESTERYEAR'S was the first name searched; it proved to be unavailable for use because of both previously registered marks and marks that were unregistered but in use and therefore valid. A second search, for THE SOUTHERN BURGER COMPANY, turned up no obvious conflicts, indicating that that name was available for use.

Of course, if you own or work for an ad agency or graphic design studio and are given the task of creating a mark for a client, you can't compel your client to hire a trademark search. However, you can make sure that you formally recommend, in writing, that your client conduct a search to "clear" the mark you suggest. Your job is to help choose a mark that works for the new product or service and, above all, doesn't cause problems. At the very least, you want to avoid being blamed for any problems that may result from the new mark. If you routinely recommend trademark searches, you won't lose the confidence of your clients because of what they perceive to be your negligence. Although it is not your *legal* responsibility to determine that any mark you propose to a client will not infringe someone else's mark, a client who has been hit with a trademark-infringement suit may fail to make that distinction. Clients will always be fickle, but trademark searches give them one less basis for deciding that you should be replaced.

All this is also true for in-house creative and marketing people, except that for them the stakes are higher. If you work for a company and are asked to name a new product or service, failing to recommend a trademark search could cost you your job. Unless you know that your company's legal department, if there is one, or an outside law firm is handling a search, recommend one at the very beginning of the trademark selection process. The least that will happen is that you will look like you are doing your job; the best result of your recommendation may be that you save your employer a great deal of money by averting an avoidable problem.

Most experienced marketing people view trademark searches as a necessary part of the process of launching new products or services. It's your obligation to point out the pitfalls inherent in ignoring the fact that adopting a trademark without investigating its availability can result in real trouble. Any professional learns that part of success in business is "encouraging" clients and employers, in a loud voice if necessary, to do what is best. This is your line: "Mr. Jones, I'm sure a man of your experience understands the necessity for a search to clear this proposed mark for use before you invest a zillion dollars in it. When may I expect to see a copy of the search report?" Nobody is happy with anybody else after any business dispute, and trademark-infringement lawsuits are likely to have everyone involved in the creation of the offending trademark pointing an accusing finger at everyone else. Luckily, you can help eliminate much of the risk in adopting a new trademark simply by remembering that the risk exists and advising your client or boss to take steps to avoid it.

Even though you need a lawyer to interpret the raw data in a trademark search report, it is possible for you, by yourself, to conduct a preliminary search to eliminate some unavailable marks early in the trademark selection process. This is possible by using a trademark directory or an online or CD-ROM trademark database.

By consulting a trademark database—in either print or electronic form—at the point in the trademark selection process when you have narrowed your choices for the new mark to three or four names, you can eliminate any marks that are already registered or are the subject of pending registration applications. This saves the expense of conducting a full trademark search for every possible name and speeds up the selection process by halting your further consideration of marks that are already registered or are soon to be registered for a product or service similar to the one for which you are selecting a mark.

A trademark directory lists trademarks that are registered and therefore already in use by someone else. Marks are listed alphabetically, according to the category of product or service they name or designate. Using a trademark directory correctly takes a little practice and requires a basic knowledge of what constitutes trademark infringement, but anybody who can use a dictionary can learn to use a trademark directory as effectively as a lawyer. A directory is most useful in the case of word marks; there are three major directories of word marks. These are the available print trademark directories:

- *The Trademark Register* includes trademarks currently registered in the U.S. Patent and Trademark Office as well as applications that are pending in the Trademark Office. Marks are listed by the class of goods or services they name and are searchable by the first word of the mark only. No information is given on owners of the marks listed. At more than 2,400 pages, the 1998 edition of *The Trademark Register* is priced at $435. It offers information current through the end of the year preceding publication. *The Trademark Register* is available from *The Trademark Register,* National Press Building, Washington, D.C. 20045 or by calling 800/888-8062 or 202/662-1233.

- *The Trademark Index* lists trademarks currently registered in the U.S. Patent and Trademark Office. Marks are listed by the class of goods or services they name and are searchable by the first word of the mark only. Information is given on owners of the marks listed. The two-volume 1998 edition of *The Trademark Index* is priced at $280. It offers information current through the end of the year preceding publication. *The Trademark Index* is available from Thomson and Thomson, 500 Victory Road, North Quincy, MA 02171-3145 or by calling 800/692-8833 or 617/479-1600.

- *The Directory of U.S. Trademarks* lists trademarks currently registered in the U.S. Patent and Trademark Office as well as applications that are pending in the Trademark Office. Marks are listed by the class of goods or services they name; the alphabetical listings include each word in the marks to enable searching by any verbal element of a mark. The 1998 edition of *The Directory of U.S. Trademarks* is $1,355. The basic fourteen-volume directory offers information current through the end of the year preceding publication. Three cumulative updates are published each year; each update is $505. *The Directory of U.S. Trademarks* is available from Thomson and Thomson, 500 Victory Road, North Quincy, MA 02171-3145 or by calling 800/692-8833 or 617/479-1600.

Print directories can be very useful in eliminating from consideration any mark that is unavailable because of a current or pending registration in the U.S. Patent and Trademark Office, but they are not updated as frequently as online and CD-ROM databases, they do not contain as much information about the marks they list, and they make searching for internal verbal elements of marks difficult. The companies that publish print trademark directories also offer online and CD-ROM search resources. Thomson and Thomson offers several levels of online and CD-ROM trademark databases; for information on available products and pricing, call its Electronic Information Services Hotline: 800/692-8833. *The Trademark Register* also offers an online searching service; call 800/888-8062 for information and rates.

Both Thomson and Thomson and *The Trademark Register* also maintain Web sites that offer information about their products and services. Thomson and Thomson's Web site address is *www. thomson-thomson.com. The Trademark Register* maintains a Web site at *www.trademarkreg.com.*

It is very important to realize that looking up a proposed trademark in a trademark directory and failing to find it listed as an already registered mark does not necessarily mean that the mark is available. The absence of a mark from the directory only means that you should proceed to the next step in the trademark clearance process, which is the full trademark search commissioned and interpreted by a lawyer. A trademark directory only short-circuits further pursuit of unavailable marks; it cannot finally clear a mark for use.

Trademark Clearance Checklist

If you carefully follow each instruction listed below, your chances of adopting a trademark that leads to a dispute or lawsuit is very small. Think of the whole clearance process as insurance against trouble that no business needs.

1. *Find out where proposed marks come from.*

Ask everyone on the task force you create to select a new trademark to propose one or more names for your new product or service. And ask them to briefly describe the sources of the names they propose. For example, for a fashion doll, "MIRANDA (after the heroine of Shakespeare's play *The Tempest*)," or, for a stuffed toy dog, "PUPSY (my best friend's dog's name in 1965)." Reject any proposed name that derives from the name of *any* commercial product or service, previously or currently in use, or the name of any person alive during this century. Further, because one of your primary goals in selecting a new trademark should be to select one that is capable of being protected and registered with the U.S. Patent and Trademark Office, eliminate any proposed name that transgresses one of the Ten Deadly Sins of Trademark Selection (statutory bars to federal trademark registration) discussed at some length in chapter 4.

2. Narrow your list of proposed marks to five or fewer marks.

Pick your favorite marks for further consideration. You can do this by polling your creative team or asking the opinion of the management of the company whose product or service the new mark will name. This is also the time for focus groups or consumer surveys regarding your proposed marks. This step allows you to put your efforts into marks that are likely to succeed from a marketing standpoint. However, don't undertake any test marketing of the new product or service under any proposed name at this point, since such marketing on even a small scale may lead to liability for the infringement of an established mark.

3. Conduct a "stop-and-go search" for each mark.

A stop-and-go search is a stage of preliminary trademark searching during which you look up each mark on your short list of proposed marks in a trademark directory, stop considering any mark that would likely infringe an established mark, and go on to the next proposed mark on your list, repeating the process. Eliminate any proposed mark that is similar to (1) any mark registered in the same class as that in which your new mark would be registered, even if the established mark is used for goods or services that are dissimilar to yours, or (2) any mark used for goods and services that are related or similar to yours, even if the established mark is registered in a different class.

Further, abandon any proposed mark that is at all similar to any famous mark, since it is possible that such a proposed mark could lead to liability under the Trademark Dilution Act, even if it is used for vastly dissimilar products or services than those named by the famous mark. At this stage of clearing a mark, "famous" can be described as any mark that is immediately recognized by 30 percent or more of your creative team. (See chapter 5 for a detailed discussion of the Trademark Dilution Act.)

4. *Find a trademark lawyer.*

Unless an attorney in your company's legal department or your regular lawyer is well versed in trademark law, find a trademark lawyer. Trademark law is a narrow specialty and most lawyers who do not regularly practice trademark law find it confusing and even infuriating. Just by reading this book you will have learned more than many lawyers know about trademark law. You wouldn't ask an auto mechanic, however competent he is, to fix your stereo—so hire the right kind of lawyer to help clear your new mark. Consult chapter 6 for tips on finding a trademark lawyer. And if you don't have one at the start of the clearance process, move this step in the process to the top of the list and begin there.

5. *Commission a trademark search.*

Have your lawyer hire a trademark search firm to conduct what is called a "full" trademark search for the most promising proposed mark on your short list. A full search is a search of the trademark records in the U.S. Patent and Trademark Office and in all the state trademark offices, and of the phone directories and trade directories and other databases that offer information on unregistered but valid marks. If you are in a real hurry, commission searches for two or three of your proposed marks at the same time so as to get the news about the availability of these marks all at once rather than searching one mark and then searching another on your short list of proposed marks if the first proves to be unavailable.

So that your lawyer may instruct the search firm correctly as to the scope of the search, make sure that you give him or her the following information:

- a copy of the proposed mark, spelled as you intend to use it. The actual verbal content of the proposed mark is very important. A word spelled one way may be available while the same word spelled in another way may not be.

- an accurate and full description of each product or service that the proposed mark will name. That is, if you intend to market action figures, comic books, a board game, and children's videos under the mark JUSTICE CRUSADERS, your memo to your lawyer on the subject would describe these products as "toy action figures, named collectively 'Justice Crusaders,' based on the characters of the 'Justice Crusaders' series of comic books, and a board game and videotapes featuring these characters." Because a trademark naming these products would have to be searched in four classes to compare it to established trademarks for goods similar to the JUSTICE CRUSADERS products, the search will be much more extensive and complicated, and generally more expensive.

- a list specifying the anticipated territories where the products to be named by the proposed mark would be marketed. Most trademark searches are of U.S. records only. This is fine, as far as it goes. However, many marketers, especially those who market easily exportable services or goods, want, at least eventually, to expand their market to other countries. If you have any plans at all for such expansion, let your lawyer know, since clearing a mark for international use involves searches of records in the other countries where it will be used. Failure to clear a mark in another country where marketing is planned can result in a suit for trademark infringement in that country, which is as much of a problem, or more, as a U.S. suit.

6. *Follow your lawyer's advice.*

Lawyers' fees buy not only legal services, but also the informed judgment that good lawyers develop over the years of their practice. Your lawyer's evaluation of the likelihood that your proposed mark will conflict with an established mark is the heart of the opinion letter that he or she will write after carefully reviewing your search report. In formulating this evaluation, your lawyer will weigh many factors, large and small, gleaned from the information in the search report. Your lawyer should try to accurately assess the chances of conflict, but most lawyers will be conservative in this assessment. If you feel that your lawyer is being overcautious in recommending that you abandon your plans to use a proposed mark, get another trademark lawyer to evaluate your search report which is, since you pay for it, yours.

Whatever you do, however, don't just ignore your lawyer's reservations and cautions about a mark. This is reportedly what the marketing department at Nike did when it named a new women's running shoe INCUBUS®. The Nike legal department had apparently advised the marketing department that the word "incubus" means "an evil spirit believed to seize or harm sleeping persons" and had recommended that another mark be chosen. Marketing ignored the advice. After the INCUBUS shoe was introduced, somebody noticed that Nike had chosen a bad name for the shoe and stories started appearing in the press. The shoes were recalled at some expense. Nike was embarrassed. It's a safe bet that the folks in Nike's marketing department wish that they had not ignored the advice of the company's trademark lawyers.

7. Register your proposed mark(s).

After you have cleared one or more of your proposed marks for use, file an intent-to-use application to register any mark that you think you may use. This serves several purposes:

- Filing an intent-to-use application, in effect, "reserves" any mark for which you file such an application. As soon as you file, your application becomes a part of Trademark Office records and will begin to turn up in other people's trademark searches, resulting in their avoidance of your proposed mark.

- Filing an intent-to-use application extends your rights in your trademark. Once you have begun to use the proposed mark and your registration application is granted, the date of first use of the mark is presumed to be the date you filed the registration application, even if that is months or even years before you actually began to use the mark. And because you can postpone the deadline for filing proof of your actual use of the mark for up to thirty-six months after the filing date of your application, you can take your time developing the new product or service the mark will name, as well as the marketing campaign for it, secure in the knowledge that no one else can register your mark before you begin to use it. If you file to register more than one mark and end up using only one, you can simply abandon the applications to register those you do not intend to use. When you decide to abandon a mark that you have previously filed to register, you will have lost only your filing fee and the fee your lawyer charges to prepare the application.

- Filing an intent-to-use application negates the biggest un-avoidable drawbacks of trademark searches. Because trademark searches report the status of the trademarks they include as of the date the search was conducted, they become out-dated quickly. This cannot be helped. Like a weather report, a trademark search that is accurate today may be inaccurate tomorrow. However, if you file an intent-to-use registration application as soon as your trademark lawyer lets you know that a proposed mark appears to be available for use, you negate the danger that the report will soon be "stale." Filing to register your proposed mark gets your name in the hat as the owner of that mark ahead of anyone else who may decide to adopt it because, when your application is eventually granted, you will be able to use, as your date of first use of the mark, the date you filed the application to register it. Priority of use is usually determinative in questions of trademark ownership, so filing an intent-to-use application can effectively eliminate any competition for ownership of your mark.

Design Trademark Clearance

A trademark can be a symbol or a name or word. The best trademarks are visually memorable, even if they are primarily verbal. Think of the familiar, distinctive-typeface trademarks for Coca-Cola®, Kleenex®, and L'eggs®. As famous as these marks are, even more effective are the symbols that immediately communicate, without words, that the products to which they are applied origi-nated with their manufacturers. A good example of this is Apple Computer's striped-apple-with-a-bite-missing logotype. Computer consumers in any part of the world are likely to recognize the Apple logo and to know that it guarantees high-quality products. In an era when many marketers aspire to market their products inter-nationally, symbol trademarks are more important than ever before.

Unfortunately, the continuing proliferation of trademarks has made it difficult to create a trademark that is safe to use.

As we have seen, in order to avoid creating trademarks that infringe existing marks, you must know something about the standard used to judge trademark infringement. Trademark infringement is evaluated by applying the "sight, sound, and meaning test." That is, the proposed mark is compared to established marks for similarities of appearance, sound when spoken, and meaning. If there are enough similarities between the proposed mark and an established mark that consumers are likely to confuse the two marks if they are used for similar goods or services, the proposed mark is said to be "confusingly similar" to the established mark and cannot be used without the risk of a lawsuit for trademark infringement. While it is easier to compare verbal marks for confusing similarity, it is equally important that the evaluation of similarities be made for trademarks whose impact is primarily visual. This group of marks includes marks that consist of a name or word that is rendered in a distinctive typeface and marks that include or consist of logotypes.

Available for Use

Obviously, when comparing design marks for similarities, the "sound when spoken" part of the three-part infringement test does not apply. However, the absence of this part of the infringement evaluation test makes the other two-thirds of the test proportionately more important. With design marks, whether you will face a federal lawsuit for trademark infringement just after spending most of your advertising budget for the year to introduce your new logo depends equally on what the logo looks like and what it "means."

The evaluation of a proposed logo starts with a consideration of the broadest possible group of established marks that are similarly configured. For instance, if Texaco were only now considering adopting its familiar five-pointed-star-in-a-circle logo, all established star and star-in-circle marks would be examined to determine if the "new" Texaco logo infringed any of them. All marks that included other prominent visual elements besides star designs could be eliminated from the universe of marks examined for confusing similarity because such additional elements would eliminate any real probability that consumers would confuse the Texaco mark with them.

Similarly, all star marks that consisted of realistic drawings of stars could be dropped from the ongoing comparison; all such logos would be dissimilar enough to the highly stylized Texaco star design to eliminate any real chance of consumer confusion. Any remaining star marks would be scrutinized carefully to judge whether the "proposed" Texaco logo would be likely to be confused with them. If such marks were used to market products or services that were remote from petroleum products or gas station services, any similarities that existed would be of less concern. However, the closer the products or services named by an established mark were to Texaco's, the more serious an impediment to the adoption of the Texaco mark the established mark would be. Even if the proposed Texaco mark were nearly identical to an established mark used to market sophisticated medical apparatus to hospitals and physicians, the hospital-equipment star trademark could be of very little concern to the petroleum company. This would depend largely on whether there was any overlap in the marketplace between the two marks; if not, they could coexist comfortably in American commerce without bumping into each other.

Image Plus Word

These same evaluations would be made in clearing for adoption and use a mark that consisted of a name or word rendered in a distinctive typeface. The difference, of course, is that there would be an additional important element in the search—the verbal content of the mark. The verbal content of a mark is usually considered to be its dominant element for purposes of comparing it to existing marks to determine confusing similarity. However, the visual impact of such a proposed mark is by no means immaterial, especially in a situation where the verbal content of the mark is not so different from that of other marks used for similar products. For example, if a shoe manufacturer adopted for its new line of ladies' shoes the name SWEET FEET and printed the mark, in a script typeface in navy blue ink, on the insoles of its products, it might encounter some opposition, in the form of a cease and desist letter, from the marketer of the SUGAR FOOT line of women's footwear, especially if the SUGAR FOOT mark were applied to SUGAR FOOT products in the same location and with the same color ink in a similar typeface. The verbal elements of these two marks do not sound alike when spoken and do not have identical meanings. However, the products they name are identical. The choice of a script typeface for the new SWEET FEET mark is all that is necessary to push SWEET FEET into "confusing similarity" territory, where the SUGAR FOOT manufacturer will have no choice but to challenge it.

The good news for the SWEET FEET graphic designer is that, although the designer may not have been consulted about the name of the new shoe line, which, of course, contributed to the problem with the SUGAR FOOT people, the designer is not helpless when it comes to protecting the Sweet Shoes Company from a trademark-infringement suit. The designer can insist on seeing the report for the trademark search that the Sweet Shoes marketing department had performed before it chose the name SWEET FEET. (And the SWEET FEET designer wants the *report*, which consists of fifty to one hundred pages of data, including reproductions of design marks, produced by a trademark search firm on similar marks already in use, rather than the opinion letter, based on the search report, written by the trademark lawyer who interpreted the report data but only in terms of the verbal elements of established marks versus those of the proposed mark.) And the designer can, using what can be learned by looking at the existing, established design trademarks in that report, steer clear of any design for the SWEET FEET name that is at all similar to any established mark with any similar meaning.

SWEET FEET, rendered in a block, serif typeface with each letter in a different bright color, may be dissimilar enough to the SUGAR FOOT mark to avoid any potential problem with the SUGAR FOOT folks, who may ignore it and never even think of calling their lawyer. This depends in part on factors that no one connected with the new mark can really predict. One such factor is the plans its owners have for the SUGAR FOOT mark. (Do they plan to expand their use of it or is it an old mark for an unprofitable line of shoes that they intend to phase out?). Another is the vigilance of the SUGAR FOOT lawyers, who may be in the habit of suing any competitor who adopts any mark that is at all similar to the Sugar Foot mark or may, instead, take a more laissez-faire approach to the inevitable elbowing between competitors that occurs in a free market economy.

The same clearance process is possible for design trademarks that include no verbal elements, but the evaluation of similarities is a little more difficult because confusing similarity may result from more subtle similarities between proposed marks and established marks. The time to perform a trademark search for a design-only mark is after the field of proposed designs has been narrowed to three or fewer logotypes. Then, unless the possible choices are all simply variations on one basic design, commission a trademark search for the first-choice design. A search of all registered and unregistered U.S. design trademarks will cost a little more than $500. The lawyer's fee for interpreting the raw data in the search report will be $400 to $500. Either way, ask to see a copy of the search report and the trademark opinion letter, but don't attempt, on your own, to decide whether your proposed logo gets the green light. By seeing the search report, you will gain valuable information about other existing marks already in use for similar goods or services, but no matter how good a marketer you are, you don't have the specialized training to also function as a trademark lawyer. If your lawyer deems the design you created unavailable for use, move on to the next proposed mark on the short list of those under consideration.

Happy Endings

A cease and desist letter, which is a nasty document that demands, under threat of being sued, that you "cease" from doing something that is claimed to violate the rights of the person or company sending the letter and thereafter "desist" from ever doing it again, is only the start of the troubles that can befall you if you make a wrong choice in choosing the design for a new trademark or fail to jump through all the hoops in the process of clearing a proposed mark for use. (A sample of a cease and desist letter is reproduced in the Appendix.) The next step after a cease and desist letter is a lawsuit that requests that the court order your products pulled from distribution in order to avoid confusing consumers and damaging the reputation of the plaintiff company by creating doubt as to the origin of its products. ("Edna, were those pumps you liked so well SWEET FEET shoes or SUGAR FOOT shoes?") Such suits are often settled out of court, but a settlement would involve your abandonment of your new mark and, probably, the payment of a sizable amount in lieu of damages the court could award. Neither scenario is likely to make you happy about having adopted a new mark.

❖

CHAPTER 4

Trademark Selection

I N ADDITION TO coming up with a new trademark that will grab the attention of consumers of your product and determining that it will not infringe an established trademark, it is important to consider whether the name or symbol you choose will be eligible for federal trademark registration.

There are two types of trademark registration: (1) state trademark registration, which is cheap and easy to obtain and confers some benefits, and (2) federal trademark registration, which is not easy to obtain, but which confers much greater benefits. Since most trademark owners want to be able to register their marks federally, that is, with the U.S. Patent and Trademark Office, we will discuss restrictions on federal trademark registration.

The federal trademark statute, which governs trademark registration, imposes certain restrictions on which marks can be granted federal registration. The inherent characteristics of the mark determine whether these restrictions will prevent the eventual registration of the trademark. The problem of these restrictions can be largely eliminated by careful avoidance of a few varieties of marks that can cause the Trademark Office to deny a registration application.

The Ten Deadly Sins of Trademark Selection

There are ten reasons the Trademark Office will deny federal registration to a trademark (other than defects in the form of the application or some other procedural problem). They are the following:

1. *The mark is confusingly similar to a trademark that is already federally registered.*

The test the Trademark Office uses to determine whether your mark is "confusingly similar" to a registered mark is the same "sight, sound, and meaning" test used by judges in trademark-infringement suits to decide whether the plaintiff does indeed have grounds to complain about the defendant's use of its name, but the only thing the Trademark Office will do to you if you adopt a name that's too close to a registered trademark is deny your application to register your name. Any liability that may be incurred by the infringing use of the previously registered mark is beyond the purview of the Trademark Office; it remains the job of the owner of the registered mark to sue you.

2. *The word or, more typically, the symbol for which registration is sought does not function as a trademark, that is, does not act in the marketplace to identify the source of the goods or services to which it is applied.*

This basis for refusing federal registration is most often cited in applications for design marks that the Trademark Office believes are being used on goods merely for purposes of ornamentation rather than in any way that indicates the source of the products. In other words, the famous JORDACHE® jeans hip pocket embroidery designs may not have achieved federal trademark registration if they had not become "distinctive of the goods," that is, if they had not begun to function to indicate to consumers that the jeans that bore them were manufactured by Jordache.

3. *The mark is "immoral, deceptive, or scandalous."*

To be rejected for registration on this ground, a name has to be blatant. Some marks that are slightly risqué make it to registration, but none that are really off-color or offensive will be granted registration. Usually mild double entendres, obscure sexual slang, and all but the most shockingly vicious phrases or symbols will pass muster with the trademark examiner who reviews your registration application, even though it is the examiner's job to try diligently to figure out why it should not be granted. Before you cry "First Amendment" and "government censorship," bear in mind that the Trademark Office will not, no matter how much it hates your trademark, tell you not to use it; the government just draws the line at registering any immoral, deceptive, or scandalous name. In any case, you should avoid any really offensive name for your product or service because consumers may object to it and may have an aversion to requesting it from retailers. Moreover, some advertising media may refuse to air or publish ads that include the offending name.

The "deceptive" part of this restriction is usually not much of a problem unless your mark is going to get you in hot water anyway. For instance, if you get the bright idea to call your line of cubic zirconia jewelry BUDGET TIFFANY because you intend to copy the famous jewelry retailer's designs and to use the same famous robin's-egg-blue packaging, the Trademark Office will deny your application to register the name on the ground that, because you have no connection whatsoever with the famous jeweler, your name is deceptive. But by the time the Trademark Office's rejection of your application reaches you, your mark will already be involved in litigation, initiated by the lawyers for Tiffany's, for the offenses of trademark infringement and trade dress infringement.

(Trademark infringement is a civil offense, which means that infringers are sued in civil courts, not brought up on criminal charges by the district attorney. Infringers pay for their transgressions in dollars, not days in jail. Which is funny, if you think about it, because if someone breaks into your apartment and steals your stereo, he can be imprisoned, but if he infringes your hard-won trademark, which is like stealing your reputation, he won't go to jail, even though his infringement of your trademark may have cost you a lot more than your stereo was worth.)

4. *The mark disparages or falsely suggests a connection with persons, institutions, beliefs, or national symbols, or brings them into contempt or disrepute.*

This restriction is similar to the "immoral, deceptive, or scandalous" restriction. For example, if you want to call your rock band TRICKY DICK in honor of the only U.S. president ever to resign from office, that's your business, but the Trademark Office may deny your application to register that name on the ground that it disparages Richard Nixon. It doesn't matter that TRICKY DICK is merely a nickname for Richard Nixon. It doesn't even matter that he is now deceased. And your arguments that Mr. Nixon's reputation would be hard to hurt aren't going to make the slightest difference to the Trademark Office.

Applications that imply nonexistent connections with particular well-known institutions will also be denied. For instance, the Trademark Office would not grant a registration to a home-security company called F.B.I. SECURITY; call your company LAW ENFORCEMENT ALARMS, though, and you may be able to register the name. Ditto for a restaurant named SEARS AND ROEBUCK, or HARVARD for scholastic aptitude tests.

And no matter how clever you think it is, the Trademark Office will refuse to register any name or logo that disparages any belief or national symbol.

If you're a group of Jewish cantors who sing traditional Jewish songs at wedding receptions you may be able to call yourselves STARS OF DAVID and convince the Trademark Office to register the name, since your use of it would not be disparaging. However, you wouldn't be able to register that name for any rock band without running into some trouble from the Trademark Office, which could reasonably interpret your use of the name or symbol as disparaging.

The same goes for crucifixes. If you manufacture and sell white chocolate crucifixes under the name IMMACULATE CONFECTIONS, don't expect the Trademark Office to allow you to register that mark. In fact, the same obstacle will be encountered by anyone who attempts to register any name or symbol dear to the adherents of any religion, including Eastern religions as well as more familiar Western belief systems.

All this is also true for "national symbols." If you apply to register as the trademark for a night club a logo depicting Uncle Sam wearing red lipstick and rouge, white theatrical makeup, and blue eye shadow, the Trademark Office will turn you down, even if your only goal in depicting Uncle Sam in such a manner is to make him look like the female impersonators who appear at your club. Your manner of using the famous American symbol will be interpreted by the Trademark Office as bringing it into contempt or disrepute.

5. *The mark consists of or simulates the flag or coat of arms or other insignia of the United States or of a state or municipality or a foreign nation.*

The American flag, for instance, belongs equally to every American citizen. Since trademark registration gives the registrant the exclusive right to use the registered mark, the trademark statute prohibits the registration of any mark that consists of the American flag. This doesn't mean you can't use the American flag as a part of your logo; you just can't register your flag logo as a trademark. (If your logo includes the American flag only as a small part of a larger design, you may be able to register the entire design by disclaiming any exclusive right in the flag portion of it.)

The same holds true for other official symbols from just about everywhere. The manufacturer of a line of women's dresses named LA FRANCE cannot register the French flag as its trademark. Nor can a restaurant called THE LONE STAR CAFÉ register the state flag of Texas as its logo.

6. *The mark is the name, portrait, or signature of a particular living individual who has not given his or her consent for use of the mark or is the name, signature, or portrait of a deceased president of the United States during the life of his or her surviving spouse, unless that spouse has given consent to use of the mark.*

The Trademark Office cannot grant exclusive rights in the name or likeness of a living person without the consent of that person. This is an easy restriction to understand. How would you feel if you woke up one morning and found that the Trademark Office had given somebody else the exclusive right to use your name for a product or service without your permission? You'd be upset, right? Well, everybody feels the same way, which is why you have to prove to the Trademark Office that any living person whose name you use as a trademark consents to that use before you can register the name.

However, you can call your outdoor-equipment shop DR. LIVINGSTONE, I PRESUME, after the famous Englishman who explored Africa, or name your line of women's cosmetics CLEOPATRA'S SECRET or bottled olive oil DA VINCI. David Livingstone, Cleopatra, and Leonardo Da Vinci were all real people, but "were" is the operative verb. They are no longer living and are, therefore, no longer in a position to object to your use, without permission, of their names or to profit themselves from such uses. (Consider, for example, SHAKESPEARE fishing rods; no one had to ask the famous bard for his permission to use his name as a trademark.)

(A caveat, however. There is something called the "right of publicity" that famous people acquire with their fame, and sometimes it can be inherited by descendants. Basically, the right of publicity is a celebrity's right to be the only person who profits from the use of her or his famous name. This means that you should not only avoid choosing as a trademark the name of any living person but should also be very careful about adopting the name or even the nickname of any famous figure who died after, say, 1900.)

Remember that this restriction applies even if you own the company that owns the trademark. Honest. Paul Newman had to give his written consent before the trademark used to market his salad dressings and spaghetti sauce, NEWMAN'S OWN®, could be registered. Ditto for Dolly Parton and the DOLLYWOOD® amusement park and Oprah Winfrey and the popular OPRAH® television show.

So much for living people. The dead presidents restriction is sort of a leftover from when companies were likely to name their products after popular politicians in an effort to appeal to the people who made the politicians popular—you know, "TEDDY ROOSEVELT MOUSTACHE WAX." This restriction is of less concern to marketers than many of the others in the Trademark Office's long list of types of unregistrable marks, but it could play a role in your choice of a name for a new product. For example, during the lifetime of Jacqueline Kennedy Onassis you could not have registered the name JFK for rocking chairs similar to the one used by the late president without her permission. The trademark statute doesn't say what happens if the dead president is female, presumably, her widower would have to consent to any use of her name. Apparently the men (they were men) who wrote our trademark statute back in the forties thought that the possibility of a woman being elected president was so slender as to be nonexistent, so they specifically worded the statute in terms of deceased male presidents.

7. *The mark is "merely descriptive" of the goods or services it names.*

Many marketing people hate this restriction and make rude noises when their lawyers remind them of it, since they believe that the more a new product name describes the product or service it names, the better a trademark it is. If you think about it, you will realize that this is not the case.

In actuality, the best trademarks are fanciful, that is, they don't mean anything much, they just capture the imagination and come to signify the particular product they name rather than being equally applicable to any product of the same kind, which is the case with marks that are descriptive. Think of KLEENEX® or EXXON® or WISK®; none of those marks mean anything as ordinary English words, but they each immediately bring to mind the specific products marketed under them.

Besides this important consideration, there is the fact that the Trademark Office almost always disallows an application to register a descriptive mark. It will not allow, by virtue of a federal trademark registration, one company to bar all others from using what are simply ordinary words to describe a product or service. If you ask yourself whether a proposed mark would tell consumers what a product or service is, or in the case of names for publications, by whom the publication is intended to be read, you can ferret out descriptive marks before they are adopted and later turned down for federal registration.

Now, it must be said that there are many trademarks that are very descriptive that are currently registered in the U.S. Patent and Trademark Office. These marks, for the most part, started out as unqualified for registration because of their descriptiveness but later, because of the fame they acquired as the products or services they named became well known, came to signify to consumers the products or services of their particular companies. In short, after a while the Trademark Office will reconsider allowing registration of descriptive marks that have achieved some fame. But at the trademark-selection stage in the history of a product, this exception to the descriptiveness restriction should not make any difference to anyone who wants to come up with a mark that won't have to work at becoming eligible for federal registration.

8. *The mark is "deceptively misdescriptive" of the goods or services it names.*

This restriction on registration is akin to some of those mentioned above, and is similarly designed to deter the adoption of misleading or distasteful trademarks. "Deceptively misdescriptive" means a mark that falsely suggests that a product or service has some characteristic that it does not indeed possess—in other words, the mark describes what it names, but falsely.

For example, LAPIS for a line of blue glass-bead jewelry would not be granted registration, since the Trademark Office would hold that the word "lapis," when used for blue jewelry not made of the semiprecious stone lapis lazuli, was a "deceptively misdescriptive" name that could mislead consumers. The same argument would apply to, say, TOP GRAIN for vinyl luggage, SILKSHIRT for women's polyester blouses, or PURE GOLD for jewelry that is merely gold-plated.

This restriction against registering deceptively misdescriptive marks is intended primarily to discourage actual attempts to mislead consumers, but it should not be disregarded if you consider choosing an ironic name. You may get the joke in your new mark, but the Trademark Office will not be persuaded to register it by the mere fact that the name is funny if it transgresses one of the trademark statute's restrictions on registrability. For example, DR. FEELGOOD'S HEALTH TONIC used for bottled beer may not be registrable, no matter how much you or consumers like the name for its wackiness.

9. *The mark is "primarily geographically descriptive or deceptively misdescriptive" of the goods or services it names.*

When the name of a product or service includes a geographic term or place name, such as the name of a river or mountain, that either tells where the product or service comes from or suggests falsely that it comes from a place that it does not, that name will run afoul of this restriction when its owner seeks to register the mark federally. The general rule has long been that if the Trademark Office can find a geographic term in any atlas or gazetteer, registration will be denied to the mark that contains it.

The reasoning behind the first part of this restriction is that if a product comes from the geographic region named in the mark, registration for one mark that includes a geographic term that is equally applicable to all products of the same sort produced in that region would unfairly deny other manufacturers the right to use the term to describe their products. For example, CARRARA STONE for marble from Italy would be unregistrable because more than one company markets marble building materials quarried from the famous deposits at Carrara and the phrase "Carrara stone" applies equally to all such products.

The reason for the second part of the restriction, that registration will be denied to any mark that suggests a nonexistent geographic origin, is similar. If the marble was not quarried in Italy at Carrara, the name CARRARA STONE would be geographically deceptively misdescriptive because it would lead consumers to a false conclusion about the origins of the stone. This restriction has more application to manufacturers of cheese, wine, bottled water, and other products tied to certain regions than it does to the marketers of most other products, but it can have an unexpected effect on the uninitiated.

The restriction on registration of geographic marks also applies to graphic representations of a state or country. If your entire logo is the map of a state or some other recognizable representation of a piece of the world, the Trademark Office will deny it registration.

Now bear in mind that you can make up fictitious place names all day long and register them as trademarks; EMERALD CITY for mobile homes or BIG ROCK CANDY MOUNTAIN for sugar cubes would be registrable. And you can use actual place names in purely fanciful ways because no one will be likely to believe that they are used to indicate the origin of a product or service; KENYA for safari-style sport clothing would be registrable and BLUE DANUBE® has long been used for a china pattern.

And remember that, as is the case with some other restrictions on registration, famous marks enjoy different rules. (Consider the country music stars, the group ALABAMA®, for example.) When a geographically descriptive name that the Trademark Office considers unregistrable comes to signify only the product or service it names, it becomes registrable because, in effect, its fame enables it to escape the anonymity inherent in a geographic name and to function as a trademark. But trademark fame is not always easy to achieve and it is a much better idea, when adopting a new mark, to choose one that won't have to outshine competing marks before achieving registrability.

10. *The mark is primarily a surname.*

Personal names have long been considered not to be inherently distinctive when used as trademarks, which is another way of saying that they are descriptive or generic and can't, in and of themselves, point to a particular source for a product.

Think of this example: there are four zillion people in the United States named Smith, so the source of SMITH'S SOCKS for children could be anyone in the country whose name is Smith. Moreover, until one SMITH'S SOCKS became well-known enough to transcend the anonymity of most surname marks, all the Smiths in the United States could market socks using their mutual surname without infringing each other's trademark rights. In other words, surname marks do not work as trademarks until they have achieved something called "secondary meaning," which is a term trademark lawyers use to mean "Everybody knows that trademark because it's so famous."

Now, obviously, there are many famous surname trademarks that have been granted federal trademark registration by the Trademark Office. That is because WATERMAN® for fountain pens, SMITH BROTHERS® for cough drops, CAMPBELL'S® for soups, LIPTON® for tea, WILSON® for sporting goods, HOOVER® for vacuum cleaners, and CRANE® for stationery are all trademarks that have risen above anonymity by virtue of having achieved strong reputations in the marketplace. Since a trademark represents the reputation of a product or service in the market, this is just a way of saying that over the years these surname marks have achieved trademark status sufficient to persuade the Trademark Office to allow their registration.

Design Elements of Marks

It is important to remember that all the restrictions on registration listed above can also apply to design trademarks or trademarks that combine graphic elements and words. You may be able to get away with registering BON VIVANT for a "parfum" that is actually manufactured in New Jersey without running into the geographically misdescriptive restriction on registration, but use a map of France as the background for the words BON VIVANT on the perfume bottle labels and the Trademark Office will reject the application to register the mark.

Similarly, although ASTRONAUT for children's pajamas would, alone, be registrable, the use, in conjunction with the word ASTRONAUT, of sketches of Alan Shepard and Sally Ride without their permission would cause the registration application to be rejected. (In addition, this use would probably result in a suit for infringement of the astronauts' right of publicity.)

A caveat. Despite having a whole book of written-down rules to operate by, the Trademark Office, like God, often moves in mysterious ways. This means that all of the above statements about what are and are not registrable trademarks are subject to some Trademark Office exceptions, whims, and inconsistencies. However, it is important to choose a trademark that can be registered, because many unregistrable marks are also all but unprotectable. That is, if you adopt an unregistrable mark, it may be next to impossible to prevent someone else from using your mark, depending on the characteristics of the mark. Use the Ten Deadly Sins of Trademark Selection list as a guideline in selecting proposed marks and leave the final opinion as to the registrability of any proposed mark to someone who pays for malpractice insurance, your trademark lawyer. You don't have to function as a trademark lawyer in order to do your job, but you can forestall a great many problems if you know a little about what you are doing when you create a new trademark.

Naming Names

Because a trademark may be unregistrable on the basis of any of the ten registration restrictions, it may seem unreasonably difficult to find a trademark that will work. It is really easier than you think, especially if you keep in mind a few principles of trademark creation.

Trademarks that are coined out of thin air or consist of existing words used in uncharacteristic ways are referred to as "arbitrary" or "purely fanciful" marks. Arbitrary or fanciful marks are the most registrable and the most effective as trademarks. Marks that are what the Trademark Office calls "suggestive" are nearly as desirable. This is not the kind of "suggestive" you think; suggestive marks are marks that call to mind—or suggest—an association related to the product they name. They imply strength or softness or freshness or flavor, depending upon the product; they are subtle marks, created by marketers and ad people who are very skilled at making artful associations. Think of TORO® lawn mowers, DOWNY® fabric softener, IRISH SPRING® deodorant soap, and ZESTA® saltine crackers. None of these marks is obvious, but we perceive nonetheless the strength of TORO lawn mowers, the softness DOWNY fabric softener imparts to laundry, the fresh scent of IRISH SPRING soap, and the zesty taste of ZESTA saltines.

The least protectable and effective marks are "descriptive" marks—they merely describe what they name. For example, THE HOT DOG SHOPPE for a café that specializes in hot dogs will immediately let everyone who sees its marquee know what sort of dinner he or she can buy there, but it is hardly memorable or distinctive. HOT DOG HEAVEN would be somewhat less descriptive. THE DOG HOUSE would be better still. HOT DIGGITY DOG would be the most memorable and registrable of all. If you think up a proposed mark that is too descriptive to register, start substituting words for some of the elements of the descriptive mark. You may be able to move the mark from "descriptive" to, at least, "suggestive" by simply using one different word.

Any method for coming up with new trademarks that works, works. However, the tips listed below are a good place to start in your quest to create a memorable and effective trademark.

Ten Tips for Creating Trademarks

1. *Assemble a creative team.*

A study of four hundred U.S. companies by Rivkin and Associates, Inc., a New Jersey marketing and consulting firm, found that the most commonly used and most effective method for finding new trademarks is a task force assembled for the purpose. These committees usually consist of someone from the company's administration, someone from marketing, a PR person, someone from sales, maybe a trademark lawyer, etc. If no one proposes such a committee, be a hero and suggest that one be formed. Several heads are better than one, and people from different disciplines bring different talents to the task of choosing a new name.

2. *Think up a name that has never existed before.*

Nobody had ever heard of EXCEDRIN® or CRAYOLA® until somebody named pain relief tablets and crayons those now-famous names. One way to create this sort of mark is to compose a long list of English-language syllables, each with a vowel and at least one consonant. Include some standard English prefixes and suffixes. Divide the list into three or four sections. Combine a syllable from the first section with any syllable from each of the other sections. Scramble the combinations you don't like, or flip them back to front. Replace syllables with others to make new combinations. Substitute a new vowel for one in a syllable that is not euphonious. Add syllables or whack them off. Be bold. It is a rule of physics that you will come up with approximately forty-seven bad combinations for every good one you stumble onto. Ignore the prevalence of bad combinations and look for the pearls.

Your working list will look like this:

RE	GO	WAN	VA
SAR	SI	CO	LA
CO	WET	MA	EY
FA	SIR	RA	MAX
DEN	SO	VA	CAM
PRO	BEN	MO	EX
NO	CA	RON	(etc.)

Your list will look like so much nonsense, and so will most of the combinations of syllables you come up with. However, play with the combinations that best roll off your tongue until you create some promising ones, then post a list of two or three over your desk and look at them for a while. Remember, the combination Co-Ca-Co-La would seem strange to anyone who had never heard of Coca-Cola®.

You can buy software programs that can help you create potential new trademarks. NamePower is available from the Decathlon Corporation in Cincinnati; call the company at 513/421-1938. Namer is available from Salinon Corporation in Dallas; the company can be reached at 212/692-9091. Neither of these programs will tell you which of the many names they generate is the best—your own taste and marketing savvy will have to do this—but they can provide you with a multitude of possibilities.

3. *Use a common word in an uncommon way.*

"Apple" once meant only a kind of fruit; now we know it also means a particular famous brand of computer. The word "windows" has gone through a similar transformation; it now signifies a particular brand of computer software while retaining all its previous meanings. Be creative. Be silly. Mine your dictionary.

4. *Use an uncommon word in a new way.*

"Oreo" is the Greek word for "hill." The original plan was to market mound-shaped cookies as Oreo® cookies. The cookies were flattened in the process of development, but the name stuck— enough so that every kid in America, and most adults, ask for these particular cookies by name. There are other familiar uses of unfamiliar words: Volvo® means "I roll" in Latin; Reebok® was the name of a particular kind of fleet-footed African gazelle before it became a brand name for running shoes; and Nike® was the name of the Greek goddess of victory long before it was the name of one of Reebok's competitors.

5. *Marry two or more words.*

Some of the most famous marks in the world were formed by constructing a new word by combining others, usually descriptive terms, either as whole words or in a truncated form. Nabisco® was formed from "National Biscuit Company" in this manner. Other examples include CITIBANK® ("city" plus "bank"), SPAM® ("spiced ham"), and NYQUIL® ("night" plus "tranquil"). One way to begin creating a mark of this sort is to list all the words you can think of that favorably describe the product you are naming. Then stick them together in combinations of two or three. Eliminate syllables here and there to create snappy combination words that are easy to say, spell, and hear.

6. *Look at the forms, shapes, and inhabitants of nature.*

Inspiration for a new trademark or logo may be as close as the seashore, the woods, the skies, or your backyard. The Texaco star logo is one of the simplest commercial designs on the cultural landscape, but it has also outlasted a lot of fussier, more pretentious logos and has for a long time signified only that company and its products to most Americans. Consult field guides and nature encyclopedias. Look at books on symbols. Study reproductions of cave paintings and hieroglyphics. Look at maps of the constellations.

Think, too, of the traditional meanings or mythological significances of certain natural objects and animals. Tradition has it that owls are wise, bulls are aggressive, lions are proud, bees are busy, turtles are slow, ants are industrious, dogs are faithful, cats are aloof, mice are quiet, and monkeys are playful. An owl logo could serve as the trademark for a textbook company. A bee logo could signify the busyness of the personnel of a housecleaning service. A monkey logo could signal visually to kids and their parents that there is fun to be had at an amusement park or a fast-food restaurant. Read Aesop's fables and the Uncle Remus tales. Peruse books of folk tales from other cultures.

7. *Study world cultures.*

Study English heraldry or Scottish tartans or Celtic symbols. Get a book on origami or Japanese art or Chinese symbols. Read Shakespeare or Chaucer (that's where Toyota got CRESSIDA®) or Bullfinch's mythology. Ask your librarian for books on African art. Find out about the Olmecs, the Toltecs, the Aztecs, the Mayas, and the Incas. Study Inuit art. Read up on other native cultures of the Americas.

More than one product has successfully borrowed the symbols or legends or literature from another culture or the past to create a memorable trademark. The famous automobile trademark THUNDER-BIRD® had its origins in the name Native Americans gave to the large woodpeckers they heard in the forests of precolonial America.

8. *Consider meanings, translations, and cross-cultural meanings.*

Browse your biggest dictionary and check your thesaurus. Both may give you ideas for names. But make sure you know the meaning and all the connotations for any word you consider using as a trademark. Remember Nike's INCUBUS? Enough said.

The famous bad example of a mark that worked in English but failed spectacularly in another market is NOVA®. "Nova" means "a star that suddenly becomes very bright"—in English. This is certainly an acceptable association for an automobile, which is what the NOVA mark named when it was introduced some years ago. However, "no va" in Spanish, means, unfortunately, "no go," which is certainly a less effective name for a car south of the border and in other countries where Spanish is spoken.

The moral to this little story is to have someone who knows languages translate your proposed mark before you start printing up your packaging materials. And don't assume that your proposed mark is safe to use because it won't be used outside the United States. More than one language is spoken here and this country shows every sign of becoming more multilingual in the future. You don't want to end up with a successful product named by a trademark that offends any segment of this society or subjects your company to ridicule. Call the languages department of the nearest large university and enlist the help of a couple of professors to check your proposed marks for hidden meanings. Better still, ask a native speaker of the language to review your mark for connotations that may not be apparent to even a scholar of that language. And if you are adopting a symbol from another culture or from history, check it out with historians of that culture and religion professors. After all, once upon a time even the swastika had no evil connotations.

9. *Stay away from initials and numbers.*

IBM®, AAA®, and CBS® are certainly well known and successful trademarks, but before those companies bowed to common usage and adopted and began to use these alternate forms of their names in addition to their more formal names, they were called INTERNATIONAL BUSINESS MACHINES®, the AMERICAN AUTOMOBILE ASSOCIATION®, and the COLUMBIA BROADCASTING SYSTEM®. The point is that trademarks comprised of initials really only work when they are derived from actual company names that have been shortened in common parlance. J&T TOWING is, by comparison, a less distinctive mark because no one knows, of course, who "J" and "T" are and were before they were reduced to their initials. The exception to this is acronym marks. Consider MADD® (Mothers Against Drunk Driving), VISTA® (Volunteers In Service To America), and NOW® (National Organization for Women). However, acronyms must be memorable to be good trademarks; this means that they should have some meaning, as acronyms, that relates to the cause or goals or product characteristics of what they name. Only the most talented marketing people can create acronym marks that are not strained or obscure.

The same goes for numbers. There are well-known number marks, but their fame may attest to the excellence of the products they name rather than to the memorability of the marks. FORMULA 409® and X-14® have established profiles in the market as names for household cleaning products, maybe because they are marketed by large companies that can afford to advertise them widely. You would do less well with "1234 BAR-B-Q SAUCE," however, especially if you didn't have the money to advertise and distribute it nationally.

10. *Misspell it in an engaging way.*

Every kid—and parent—knows TOYS "R" US®, even though the company will never win an award for grammar. JELL-O® is a fractured form of "gelatin." NYTOL® is a creative rendering of "Night, all." And L'EGGS® is a "French" form of "legs." Marks that are spelled in unusual ways can be memorable because they approach the novelty of coined marks. However, there is nothing more old hat than a too-cute misspelling used as a brand name. No examples of these marks are necessary; you can see them in any grocery store.

If all else fails, suggest the given name of the CEO's child—but only as a last resort. SARA LEE® baked goods and WENDY'S® hamburgers immortalized those two little girls, but not even Ford likes to think about EDSEL® automobiles anymore.

CHAPTER 5

Trademark Protection

O NCE YOU HAVE settled on a mark, chosen from a list you or your ad agency proposed after careful consideration of the aforementioned dreaded Ten Deadly Sins of Trademark Selection, and have conducted a trademark search to determine whether the mark is available for use, the next step is the registration of the trademark. Every trademark wants to be registered after it is born. Any company that is serious enough about a new mark to spend any time or money developing it and clearing it for use will want to file as soon as possible for federal trademark registration, which means registration of the trademark in the U.S. Patent and Trademark Office, in Washington, D.C. (Ignore the fact that the name of the office includes the word "patent"; the Trademark Office and the Patent Office are entirely separate government departments that were mistakenly joined at the hip by a Congress that got confused and thought that they had something to do with each other.)

Federal Trademark Registration

The federal trademark statute, the Federal Trademark Act of 1946 (also called the Lanham Act), gives to the U.S. Patent and Trademark Office, which is a division of the Department of Commerce, the power to regulate the registration of trademarks that are used in interstate commerce or commerce between the United States and another country. The Trademark Office consists of several divisions, each of which handles a different function; most trademark owners will never be concerned with any but one of the various offices that reviews, or "examines," applications to ascertain whether registration will be granted.

There are now two types of federal trademark registration: (1) the use-based application, which is based on current use of the trademark in interstate or international commerce, and (2) the intent-to-use application, which is based on a "bona fide intent" to use the mark in interstate or international commerce. At one time, every U.S. trademark application was based on current use of the mark; since a change in the law, this is no longer the case.

Use-Based Applications

There are several requisite elements for a use-based federal trademark registration application. These include the following: the written application in proper form; a "drawing" sheet, on which the mark is reproduced according to the Trademark Office's specifications; your declaration, made under penalty of perjury, that you believe that you (or your company) own your mark and are entitled to register it; a date of first use of the mark anywhere; a date of first use of the mark in interstate or international commerce; a description of the goods or services marketed under your mark; specimens of ads, packaging, labels, etc., proving your use of your mark; and the proper filing fee, which is (at this writing) $245 per class of goods or services.

When your registration application is received by the Trademark Office mailroom, it is preliminarily reviewed for its sufficiency as an application, i.e., whether it includes all the components necessary to allow the examination process to proceed, and is given a serial number. (If you have omitted one or more important elements of your application, it will be returned.) This serial number remains the way the application is identified throughout the process of examination to ascertain whether a registration will be granted. After assignment of a serial number, your registration application is forwarded to the correct law office within the examining section of the Trademark Office and is assigned to an examining attorney. Most applicants include a self-addressed, stamped postcard in their application packets; this postcard will be stamped with the serial number and immediately mailed back to the applicant. The official filing receipt will follow, but the postcard lets you know some weeks earlier that your application was received and what serial number it was assigned.

The Trademark Office classifies all goods and services according to the International Schedule of Classes of Goods and Services; this schedule is included in "Basic Facts About Trademarks," which is reproduced in the appendix to this book. The descriptions of goods and services may seem unfamiliar. For example, the REVERE WARE® trademark is registered in International class 11, which includes "apparatus for lighting, heating, steam generating, cooking, refrigerating, drying, ventilating, water supply, and sanitary purposes." The lists of goods registered in other categories are sometimes longer. The Trademark Office examining offices are numbered: Law Office 1, Law Office 2, etc. Each law office handles all the applications made in the classes of goods or services assigned to that office. Each application is handled by one examiner, who is a lawyer, according to the provisions of the *Trademark Manual of Examining Procedure*. The examining procedures are logical and are designed to carry out the intent of the Lanham Act, but the logic of examiners' decisions is not always apparent to applicants.

Other than filing receipts that notify them of the serial numbers assigned to their applications, most applicants will receive no word from the Trademark Office for several months. The first communication you receive from the examining attorney assigned to handle your application may be a rejection of your application to register your mark.

It is an extremely common occurrence that an examiner will, at least initially, reject an application on one or more bases. The simplest such basis is that the examiner points out a small technical problem with the form of the application and suggests a small change in the language of the application to correct some technicality, such as asking for a clarification of the description of goods or services named by the mark; sometimes this sort of small amendment can be authorized by the applicant in a phone call to the examiner.

A more difficult sort of rejection to overcome is a substantive rejection based on the failure of the mark to meet one or more of the legal requirements for registration. Substantive rejections are commonly based on the trademark examiner's decision that a mark embodies one of the statutory grounds for denial of registration; for example, that it is confusingly similar to a registered mark or that it is descriptive or deceptively misdescriptive of the goods or services it names. (See the Ten Deadly Sins of Trademark Selection in chapter 4 for the entire list of statutory grounds for rejection of an application.) The reason or reasons for the rejection will be described, and one or more Trademark Office rules or court decisions in trademark cases will be cited to support the examiner's rejection of the application. Whatever the examiner's objections, the applicant has six months to respond to the rejection. Such responses answer questions the examiner may have raised and present counterarguments to the grounds cited for rejection of the application, as well as amending the application to clear up technical problems. Even if your application is initially rejected on a substantive ground, it is possible to persuade the examiner that registration should be granted. However, this can be difficult or impossible, depending on the ground for rejection. Further, this is not a do-it-yourself job.

Like all documents filed with the Trademark Office in the process of pursuing a registration, responses to rejections must fulfill strict requirements in order to suffice. Filing an application to register a trademark is like appearing in a regular court and asking the judge to rule in your favor; the applicant states that he or she believes the mark that is the subject of the application is entitled to registration under the law, presents evidence sufficient to prove that to the Trademark Office, and answers questions and presents arguments to support the granting of the registration. These are difficult procedures that take lawyers years to master. Even an application that is eventually granted can require several carefully composed replies to the Trademark Office.

If, even after you present arguments to overcome the examiner's denial of registration, your application is "finally" rejected by the examiner, there are several courses open to you. You can simply abandon your effort to register your mark, which will not affect whatever rights you have or will gain in it. You can file an appeal with the Trademark Trial and Appeal Board, which is a complicated formal undertaking somewhat like appealing an ordinary court case after an adverse verdict of the trial court. Or you can amend your application to ask that registration be granted on the Supplemental Register rather than the Principal Register (see the discussion below for an explanation of the difference between the two types of registration).

If your application is not rejected or if you overcome the examiner's initial rejection of your application, the trademark examiner is satisfied that your trademark is entitled to registration. Your trademark will then be subjected to the next step in the process of qualifying for registration. It is "published for opposition." This means that your mark is reproduced (in the case of purely verbal marks, this means only that it is printed to show its exact verbal content) in the *Trademark Official Gazette*, which is published weekly. Anyone who believes that registration of your mark will harm him or her has thirty days to file an objection to the registration, called an "opposition." Many opposition proceedings are settled; some are fought hard through the Trademark Office's in-house court, called the Trademark Trial and Appeal Board. If no one objects to the granting of your registration within the prescribed period, a certificate of registration will be mailed to you as soon as the Trademark Office's slow machinery can produce one. The whole registration process can literally take years, especially if there are rejections to be countered or if an opposition proceeding is filed. Even applications that encounter no such problems routinely take a year or eighteen months to result in a registration.

There are two varieties of federal trademark registrations: an applicant may be granted a registration on either the Principal Register or the Supplemental Register. Principal Register registrations bestow the most benefits and are the goal of every federal trademark applicant. (When the term "federal registration" is used in this book, registration on the Principal Register is meant.) However, if a mark is unable to qualify for the Principal Register, a Supplemental Register registration also has its uses. Most marks on the Supplemental Register are descriptive, surname, or geographic marks that do not yet function as trademarks, in the eyes of the Trademark Office. That is, they do not point to *one* source for the goods or services they name because they are not distinctive and have not yet acquired the degree of fame necessary to result in "secondary meaning." Marks registered on the Supplemental Register are entitled to use the ® notice of registration and gain some benefits of federal registration, such as access to federal courts, and are presumed, after a period of five years, to have gained enough fame to qualify for an upgrade (upon request by the registrant) to the Principal Register.

Intent-to-Use Applications

Once upon a time in America, it was necessary for trademark owners to have used their trademarks in interstate commerce before applying for federal trademark registration, and trademark rights began to accrue from the date a trademark owner actually began to use a mark in the marketplace. However, since November of 1989, a trademark owner can apply for registration before actually beginning to use the new trademark, so long as the trademark owner has a "bona fide intent" to begin to use the mark in interstate commerce within six months of the date the registration application is filed. (The period of time for beginning use of the mark may be extended, in six-month increments and upon making the proper filings, to a total period of thirty-six months.) Registration may then be granted after use of the mark is made in interstate commerce.

This system of registration represents a big change in the law. It is not quite the same as the system that exists in certain European countries, which allows marketers to "reserve" a trademark for use before actually adopting it, but it is close, since now U.S. companies can put everyone on notice that they intend to use a mark before they actually do so. This change should eliminate the situation that formerly existed, where two companies that had to begin using their new marks before they applied for trademark registration began to use the same mark for similar products—each discovering the existence of the other only upon filing their applications, after they had expended the time and money necessary to launch a new mark. In this situation, only one of the two companies could end up owning and registering the mark—the company that began using it first.

Now, when a company files an intent-to-use application to register a mark, stating that it will begin using the mark within six months, its intentions become part of the official records maintained by the Trademark Office and are included in the data searched by trademark search firms. This means that when a second company conducts a search to ascertain the availability of the mark, the first company's application for that mark, indicating that it has already "staked a claim" to the mark, will appear in the search report and warn the second company away from the mark.

Intent-to-use applications confer one other benefit on trademark owners that was not formerly available: when a registration is eventually granted to an intent-to-use applicant, the applicant trademark owner's rights in the mark are deemed by the new rules to commence from the filing date of the application to register, rather than just from the date of the applicant's first actual use of the mark. This means that early filing of a trademark registration application can now give additional months or even years of ownership rights, on the front end of the ownership period, to a trademark owner who had not even begun to use the mark on the date of filing.

All this complicated stuff boils down to this for businesspeople: you should know that it is possible to file for federal trademark registration just as soon as a search has cleared a new mark for use. Speed is important because the earlier the date of filing, the sooner ownership rights in the mark will, eventually, be deemed to have begun. In addition, early filing removes some of the danger that two companies will be competing for registration and ownership of the same mark.

Intent-to-use applications require essentially the same components as use-based applications. However, instead of a declaration that the mark that is the subject of the application was first used in interstate commerce on a certain date, the statement in an intent-to-use application is that the applicant has a bona fide intent to use the mark for the goods or services specified. Further, there is no requirement that specimens of use of the mark be furnished until the applicant is able to file a "Statement of Use" attesting to the fact that the mark has begun to be used in interstate commerce.

Maintaining Your Registration

Federal trademark registrations endure for a term of ten years. However, because all trademark rights are based on use of the mark, between the fifth and sixth anniversaries of the date a registration is granted, the registrant must formally attest to continuing use of the mark by filing an affidavit describing that use and furnish a new specimen of use of the mark. Further, at the end of the initial ten-year registration period, but no sooner than six months prior to the end of the period, you may file to renew your registration. You may renew the registration for your mark at ten-year intervals as many times as you want, so long as you continue to use the mark. In theory, a trademark can live in perpetuity in the marketplace. There are some trademarks that are still active after a hundred years or more of service in commerce.

Apply at Your Own Risk

It is one thing to know that federal trademark registration is desirable and to know something about the registration process, but filing for federal trademark registration is, like searching a trademark to clear it for use, not a do-it-yourself project. The Trademark Office allows trademark owners to file their own applications for registration, without the help of a lawyer, but satisfying the complicated filing requirements imposed by the Trademark Office is not easy and filing without the help of a trademark lawyer is likely to result in the rejection of the application. Lawyers do have their uses; filing for trademark registration is one of them.

However, for the brave, the registration forms prescribed by the Trademark Office are reproduced in the Appendix of this book in the reprinted pamphlet "Basic Facts About Trademarks," along with instructions for filling them out, the International Schedule of Classes of Goods and Services, and information on Trademark Office services that may be useful to do-it-yourself applicants. Remember that even if you manage to meet the requirements of the Trademark Office for a registration application, you may still be confronted with the need to keep your application on track by filing a response to some complicated objections to registration raised by the trademark examiner who reviews and evaluates your application. That is, even if you manage to file a proper application without a trademark lawyer, you still may need to consult chapter 6 to find one, because almost no one who has not done it before can successfully respond to a complicated Trademark Office rejection of an application. Failure to respond will result in the abandonment of your application; failure to respond *fully* will result in a final rejection of your application.

Federal trademark registration offers several important advantages to trademark owners, among them:

- A federal registrant has rights in the registered mark superior to anyone else except prior users of the mark.
- The owner of a federally registered trademark is in a much better position to quash infringers than if the mark were not registered, since federal registration offers immediate access to a federal court, where a federal registrant can obtain an injunction with nationwide effect to stop infringers.
- A federal trademark registrant who sues an infringer in federal court may be entitled to recover profits, damages, and court costs, including attorney's fees. In some circumstances, the registrant may be awarded "treble damages," which are damages three times the amount that would ordinarily be awarded.
- Moreover, because a federal registration gives the registrant the benefit of the presumptions that the registrant owns the registered mark and that the registration is valid, registrants who end up in court have a powerful advantage over any challenger who also claims ownership.
- A federal registration serves as "constructive notice" to any subsequent user of the registered mark that the registrant

claims ownership of it. In other words, the presence of the registration in the public records of the Trademark Office is presumed to make any other would-be user of the mark aware of prior ownership claims of the registrant. This eliminates any defense raised by an alleged infringer that the mark was adopted in good faith.

- After five years, a registered mark may become "incontestable"; that is, the registration becomes conclusive evidence of the registrant's right to use the mark.

Even better, federal trademark registration helps trademark owners avoid the necessity of bringing suit to stop trademark infringers in two important ways. First, once a trademark is registered in the Trademark Office, any other companies that conduct searches to clear proposed new marks will know that the registered mark is already in use for the goods and services it names and will stay clear of it or any confusingly similar mark. Secondly, even if some company does infringe the mark, it is likely to agree to stop using the mark immediately upon the receipt of a cease and desist letter from the trademark owner's lawyer, since the infringer will know that the owner of the registered mark does, indeed, have the clout to prevent the continued infringing use of the mark. These circumstances have the effect of stopping trademark-infringement lawsuits at the optimum time—before they start.

Notice of Registration

Once a trademark is registered federally, and this means registered in the U.S. Patent and Trademark Office, not simply registered in one or more states or in another country, the trademark owner is allowed to use, and should use, a trademark registration notice in conjunction with the registered mark. Use of such notice warns others that the mark is registered and that ownership of it is claimed by the owner, and allows the owner to gain certain advantages provided by the federal trademark statute.

The most familiar trademark registration notice is the "circle R" symbol, or ®; the ® symbol should be used "on the shoulder" of the registered mark (in the superscript position), or in the subscript position, very near it. Alternate forms of notice are "Registered in the U.S. Patent and Trademark Office," or "Reg. U.S. Pat. & Tm. Off."; these alternate forms of notice should be used with an asterisk placed close to the registered mark and a corresponding asterisk preceding the notice itself, which usually appears in a footnote position on the package or label or in the ad, etc.

It is important to know that the forms of trademark notice specified above are the only forms of notice that have the legal effect of proper trademark registration notice. You can't, in short, make up your own.

Not using the ® symbol (or one of the other prescribed forms of trademark registration notice, although they are generally used less often and may, in fact, be less likely to be recognized as notice of registration than the familiar ® symbol) in conjunction with a federally registered trademark will not invalidate the registration, but it can deprive the trademark owner of some very important advantages in the event that the registered mark is infringed.

If the Rounder Doughnut Company registers its trademark HOLE IN ONE for packaged doughnuts sold in grocery stores, everyone else in the world who wishes to adopt and use in the United States a confusingly similar trademark for doughnuts is presumed by law to have notice that HOLE IN ONE is owned by Rounder, even if they do not conduct a trademark search and discover Rounder's federal registration. If Burgerama, Inc., adds to the breakfast menu for its fast food restaurants a doughnut it calls HOLE IN ONE, the Rounder Doughnut Company will sue Burgerama, since consumers could easily confuse the fast food restaurants' doughnuts with those marketed by Rounder. By virtue of its federal registration, Rounder will be entitled to an injunction from the court ordering Burgerama to cease use of HOLE IN ONE.

But if Rounder also wants to be awarded an amount of money representing the damages it has suffered because of Burgerama's infringement or the profits of Burgerama attributable to the sale of doughnuts under the HOLE IN ONE name before its receipt of Rounder's cease and desist letter, Rounder must have used the ® symbol (or another prescribed form of notice) on its packaging. If Rounder did not use a trademark registration notice with its mark, the court is allowed by law to award only damages or profits that resulted from actions of Burgerama *after* it received actual, specific notice that the HOLE IN ONE mark was registered.

Now all this may sound like mumbo jumbo, but it's not. It may seem unlikely that something that a commercial artist does or does not do in pasting up the artwork for a new cereal box or an ad for a vacuum cleaner can determine how much money a federal court can award to the cereal company or the vacuum cleaner company, but that is precisely the case.

The responsibility to make sure that a trademark registration symbol is properly used with a registered trademark belongs ultimately to the trademark owner. If you are not the owner of a trademark or responsible for managing a company that owns it, you have no legal obligation to find out whether a trademark owned by your client or your employer is registered or to make sure that the trademark registration symbol is used. However, no client or employer is going to object to your raising the question of the proper use of a registered mark. If you want to keep your clients or employer happy, you must be at least conversant with the basics of proper usage of the trademark registration symbol and notations, since that usage so directly affects valuable rights of trademark owners.

An important related consideration is the improper use of the ® symbol (or another of the prescribed forms of trademark registration notice). If trademark registration notice is used in conjunction with a trademark that is not federally registered, or used with a trademark appearing in advertising for, or in conjunction with, goods or services for which it is not registered, serious consequences can result, including the loss of the trademark owner's right to recover for trademark infringement or to register the mark federally.

Many people, even people who should know better, think that the ™ symbol they often see printed next to trademarks is the equivalent of the ® symbol and has some legal effect. In reality, it does not. The ™ symbol is sometimes used by trademark owners as a "no trespassing" sign to indicate that someone is claiming ownership of the mark. It has no real legal effect but can be useful, since there are no requirements to be met before it can be used and there really is no such thing as misuse of it. In addition, many trademarks are not yet federally registered, or have been denied federal registration, or cannot be federally registered for one reason or another. Use of the

™ symbol, which usually appears in the same locations as those used for placement of the ® symbol, can warn others that the owners of these names consider them to be trademarks and claim ownership of them. (Another form of informal trademark notice, the ᔆᴹ symbol, is often used in the same ways that the ™ symbol is used when the mark in question names services.)

Similar to the ™ symbol is some statement such as "The name DENTAL ASSISTANT'S QUARTERLY is a trademark of the Dental Assistance Association of America." Statements of this sort have exactly the same effect (some) and uses (several) that the ™ symbol does; that is, they are another variety of informal trademark notice.

State Trademark Registration

We will consider state trademark registration only briefly, for two reasons. First, state trademark registration offers much less protection to a mark than federal registration. Second, state registrations do not involve nearly so many rules and regulations as federal registrations and are usually easy to obtain.

You can almost certainly handle state registration of your trademark without a lawyer. The first thing to do is to call or write the trademark department of the state in which you want to register your mark. (State trademark departments are usually part of the secretary of state's office; you can find a list of these agencies for each state in the appendix.) Request a printed trademark registration form. These are always free. When the form arrives, carefully read it and the instructions that will come with it, fill in the blanks, sign it, send it back with the proper application fee (not much; fees vary from about $10 to $25, depending on the state) and with the specimens of use of the mark required. You will have to specify in what class of goods or services you want to register your mark. This will be one of the classes of the old U.S. classification system for trademarks. You will be sent a copy of this list of categories with your blank registration application.

All the states have some sort of trademark statute; most are based on a model trademark statute. The provisions of state trademark statutes largely echo those of the federal statute. However, the federal trademark statute only applies to trademarks that are used in interstate commerce. The state statutes are designed to regulate the use of trademarks and protect the rights of trademark owners within each state.

Although some states offer more protection to trademark registrants than others, it is never a bad idea to apply for and secure a state registration for your trademark. Among other benefits, state trademark registration:

- documents your ownership of your mark before you have used it in interstate commerce and are able to apply for federal registration,
- offers protection against infringement within the state where your mark is used, and
- causes your mark to show up in the trademark search reports other people commission.

You can apply for state trademark registration only in the state or states where you are currently using the mark. As with federal registration, "use" of a mark in a specified territory is defined as the offering for sale of the product to which the mark is applied or the advertising of and readiness to offer the services the mark names.

A good strategy is to apply for state registration for your mark as soon as you begin using it. This may be before you have begun to use the mark in interstate commerce or concurrent with your use of the mark in interstate commerce. You should file a federal use-based application or intent-to-use application at the same time. File to register the mark in every state where you are using it; apply to register your mark in additional states when you expand your use of your mark to those states. This plan will give you as much protection as possible as early in the life of your mark as possible, at the lowest possible cost.

In most cases, state trademark registrations endure from five to ten years. As with federal registrations, you must renew state registrations prior to the expiration of the initial term of registration. If you have secured federal registration for your mark since filing for state registration and the federal registration is current and in effect at the end of the initial term of state registration, you can safely let your state registration lapse, since a federal registration offers much broader protection.

Even if your mark is only registered in one or more states, you should be careful to follow the rules for proper use of trademarks discussed in chapter 7. However, do not use the ® symbol or any other form of notice that indicates federal trademark registration until and unless your mark is registered federally. Ignoring this restriction on the use of notice of federal registration can seriously damage your right to stop infringers or later register your mark with the U.S. Trademark Office. Use the ™ (or ℠) freely, but stay away from the ® symbol unless you have earned the right to use it by virtue of having been granted a federal registration.

New Protection for Famous Marks

Owners of famous trademarks gained substantial new protection from the federal Trademark Dilution Act of 1995, which was signed into law by the president and became effective in January of 1996. The act formalizes and makes a part of the federal trademark statute a principle of trademark law that had been available as a ground for suit in only about half the states. It allows the owners of an existing "famous" trademark to ask the court to enjoin the use of the same mark by another company—even if there is no likelihood of confusion between the marks—on the ground that the defendant's use of the mark, even for noncompeting goods or services, "dilutes" the distinctive quality of the famous mark. This allows the owners of truly famous marks to stop the use of their marks by the marketers of noncompeting goods and services as well as by competitors. One of the first lawsuits brought under the new act was initiated by Hasbro, Inc., which owns the trademark CANDY LAND® for the famous children's board game, against a company that had adopted the domain name candyland.com for a sexually explicit Web site. Hasbro was successful in having the domain name enjoined on the basis that its use would dilute the strength of the CANDY LAND mark. Other, similar cases have followed. A recent example is the suit brought by Federal Express to halt the use of FEDERAL ESPRESSO as the name of a Syracuse coffeehouse.

The new act defines "dilution" as "the lessening of the capacity of a famous mark to identify and distinguish goods or services, regardless of the presence or absence of (1) competition between the owner of the famous mark and other parties, or (2) likelihood of confusion, mistake, or deception." Although most really famous marks are registered in the U.S. Patent and Trademark Office, federal registration is not a prerequisite for protection of a mark under the act, which protects registered and unregistered marks equally, given an equal degree of fame.

The Trademark Dilution Act enumerates several factors to be considered in evaluating whether the mark owned by a plaintiff in a suit under the act really is distinctive and famous enough to be protected under its provisions. These include the following:

- the degree of inherent or acquired distinctiveness of the "famous" mark,
- the duration and extent of use of the "famous" mark,
- the duration and extent of advertising and publicity for the "famous" mark,
- the geographical extent of the trading area in which the "famous" mark is used,
- the channels of trade through which the product or service named by the "famous" mark is sold,
- the degree of recognition of the "famous" mark in the trading areas and channels of trade used by both the owner of the "famous" mark and the defendant against whom the injunction is sought,
- the nature and extent of any use by third parties of marks that are the same as or similar to the "famous" mark, and
- whether the owner of the "famous" mark has a valid federal registration.

These factors are not exclusive; that is, they are specifically not the only factors that may be considered.

For most trademark owners, the Trademark Dilution Act will not offer any more protection than the federal trademark statute offered before the new act was passed. This is understandable; very few marks can hope to reach the level of fame required to trigger protection from trademark dilution under the new law. For an understanding of the sort of fame that courts are likely to require before invoking the penalties of the new law, we have only to look to the LEXIS® case, decided not long before the new act was passed.

The manufacturer of the automobile LEXUS® was sued by the owners of the online legal research service LEXIS on the ground of dilution. LEXIS lost. The court held that LEXIS was not well-known enough outside the legal community to have suffered dilution at the hands of the automobile manufacturer. In other words, the sort of fame necessary to support a claim of trademark dilution is what used to be known as becoming "a household word." When the great majority of consumers are aware of a mark and the products or services it names, it is "famous" in the sense meant by the Trademark Dilution Act. If only some people are aware of the mark, or if almost everyone in a certain profession or industry is aware of it but practically no one outside that group is, the mark has not (yet) achieved the degree of fame necessary to command this very broad protection under the law.

Most marketers need only remember that a long-standing guideline for trademark selection is even more important since the passage of the Trademark Dilution Act. "Stay away from famous marks" is better advice than ever. Now owners of famous marks have a more direct and powerful way to stop you from naming your motor oil COORS® or your line of kids' clothing CHEERIOS®.

The new statute specifies several legitimate uses of famous trademarks that will not create any liability under the law. These exclusions from the proscriptions of the act are a response to legitimate First Amendment concerns. The new act expressly exempts:

- fair use of a mark in comparative advertising,
- parody, satire, editorial commentary, and other noncommercial uses of a mark, and
- any form of news reporting or commentary that mentions a mark.

(See chapter 8 for a more detailed discussion of the use of trademarks that belong to others.)

❖

Trademark Laywers

I N A WORLD where people find their mates through newspaper ads, it is not surprising that businesspeople sometimes select their lawyers from the Yellow Pages. Like marriage, the relationship between lawyer and client is often contracted with too little thought. Of course, your relationship with your lawyer isn't as important as marriage, but when you choose a lawyer to handle a legal matter, you do entrust an important part of your life to him or her for a while. This means that you should use at least as much care in selecting your lawyer as you devoted to buying your last car.

This is especially true with regard to any legal matter related to trademarks. Trademark law is a narrow area of the law about which most lawyers are content to remain ignorant, because it is confusing and sometimes even infuriating and resembles semantics more than it does other areas of the law. Very few lawyers who do not regularly practice trademark law are competent to handle even the most minor trademark matter. This means that you will need a *trademark* lawyer whenever you are confronted with any of the following situations:

- when you choose a new trademark,
- when you expand the use of an existing trademark to additional products or services,
- when you file for federal trademark registration,
- when you believe that someone is infringing your trademark rights,
- when you are accused of infringing someone else's trademark, and
- when you want to license your trademark to someone else.

The first thing to know about finding a lawyer is that the lawyer referral services offered by local bar associations are practically worthless. These services include many fine lawyers in their listings, but they also include more than a few lawyers who are badly educated, inexperienced, predatory, unethical, or all of the above. This is because these services ordinarily refer callers, on a rotating basis, to lawyers who are members of the bar associations that sponsor them, without attempting to evaluate the abilities of the attorneys who are listed. You may be referred to a lawyer who has signed up for the referral service as a "trademark lawyer," but that is probably the lawyer's own evaluation, so you really won't know how extensively the lawyer has practiced trademark law or what level of competence he or she has reached. In other words, these services really offer no more information to the consumer than the Yellow Pages.

Most bar associations are like clubs; usually, such an association will accept as a member any lawyer who will pay the association's annual dues and is licensed to practice law where the association is located. The fact that a lawyer possesses a license to practice law is *not* enough to ensure that he or she will give you the help you need in handling a particular matter or treat you fairly. A law license means only that the lawyer who holds it graduated from a law school, passed a character review and the bar exam for the state that issued the license, and has not been disbarred since.

There's a big difference between being the kind of lawyer everyone wants to hire and simply avoiding disbarment. A lawyer with a valid law license may have graduated at the bottom of his class from an unaccredited law school and have passed the bar exam only on the third try. She may be inexperienced, inept, ignorant, and disorganized. He may be an alcoholic or a drug addict. She may be dishonest or greedy. However, unless these failings have so harmed a client that the client filed a formal complaint with the licensing body in the state where the lawyer practices and that body found, after investigation, that the lawyer should be suspended or disbarred, he or she can hang a valid law license on the wall and continue to accept new clients.

Another poor method for finding a lawyer is lawyer advertising. Some good lawyers advertise. However, many lawyers who hawk their services through broadcast and print ads run their practices like factories. You are unlikely to get much individual attention from one of these lawyers. And although the content of lawyer advertising is regulated to some extent, ads for lawyers, which often depend on cheap theatrics for their effect, are really no more reliable than any other sort of advertising. That is, they *may* advertise the services of competent, trustworthy lawyers, but there's no way to tell from the ads whether they actually do. Further, it is unlikely that most firms that advertise will employ any lawyer who is qualified to practice in a highly specialized area such as trademark law.

This means that you should find your trademark lawyer through some means other than the Yellow Pages, a bar-association referral service, or lawyer advertising. These are the easiest methods for locating a lawyer, but they are also the least effective in terms of finding a good one who is suitable for your needs. Compiling a list of trustworthy, qualified lawyers requires some work, but, after all, either the matter for which you need a trademark lawyer is important enough to approach seriously, with some forethought, or it isn't. If you are not willing to expend the time and effort that such an initial screening process requires, you should reconsider whether you really want to pursue a legal solution to your problem or would rather forget the whole thing. There are several ways to come up with a list of good trademark lawyers; none of them is especially difficult.

Perhaps the best way to find a competent, ethical trademark lawyer is to call a lawyer you know and trust for help. If you already have a relationship with a lawyer you like who doesn't practice trademark law, ask that lawyer to recommend three other lawyers who *are* qualified to help you. Most lawyers within a city know, or can find out, which other lawyers are considered able, honest, and experienced in their fields, even if they are not familiar with the specialized work of those other lawyers. And a lawyer whose client you have been and whom you trust is likely to be careful in making such recommendations; in fact, if you ask a lawyer for three or four names and he or she responds with only one or two, he or she is being scrupulous by refusing to refer you to someone about whom he or she knows too little.

The best referral is from a lawyer who personally knows the lawyers to whom he or she refers you. This is because most lawyers will be especially careful of their treatment of a client when they know—or think—their actions are likely to be judged by another lawyer. However, a subclass of lawyer referrals to watch out for is the referral to another lawyer in the same firm. It is very possible that the lawyer to whom you are referred under such circumstances will be a paragon of skill and knowledge. It is also possible that you will be referred to a lawyer in the same firm simply because the referring lawyer is more concerned with the firm's income than with your getting the best possible recommendation. Don't reject such referrals out of hand, but make your own judgments. Nothing obligates you to engage the services of any lawyer to whom you are referred—lawyers speak of "their" clients; in reality, their clients should think of "their" lawyers, because the client is the person who calls the shots, although many lawyers forget this fact of capitalism.

If you don't know a lawyer who can recommend one or more trademark lawyers to you, ask several other people whose opinions you respect for a similar list of lawyers. But don't only ask your friends; even if they are true-blue, they may have very little information concerning trademark lawyers. Instead, ask other businesspeople in your town, especially those who own or manage businesses similar to yours. They may have had to solve trademark problems themselves.

Ask three questions of everyone you approach for names of lawyers: (1) How do you know these lawyers?" (2) "What do you know about them?" and (3) "Why do you think one of them could help me?" Enter the name of any lawyer who is recommended by a reliable source on your master list. After you have three or four names of trademark lawyers, start investigating them.

You probably want to hire a trademark lawyer near you. Although it is easier to work with a local lawyer, trademark lawyers are urban creatures and are seldom found outside sizable cities. You may not be able to find one near you. However, since trademark practice is mostly a matter of specialized paperwork, it is likely that you can successfully manage your lawyer's work through the mail and on the phone, at least after your initial meeting. It is also possible that you will need to hire a lawyer in the same locale as that where suit has been brought against you or where you want to sue someone else. The matter of venue in trademark lawsuits is influenced by several factors, so if you are involved in a trademark dispute, one of your first questions to any lawyer you interview is whether he or she is located and licensed in the right place to defend or bring a suit for you. Any trademark lawyer can handle trademark searches and registrations or other matters in the Trademark Office in Washington, D.C., from anywhere in the United States. This means that a trademark lawyer you hire to advise you in these matters can live near you or in another city altogether—it really doesn't matter.

Your primary tool for investigating the lawyers recommended to you is the *Martindale-Hubbell® Law Directory*. All law libraries, most law firms, and the larger branches of many public libraries own this directory, which is a series of fat volumes, organized by state and city, that list U.S. law firms. To earn a Martindale-Hubbell listing, a law firm must meet certain experience requirements and must be recommended by other lawyers who practice in the same locality.

Lawyers use the *Martindale-Hubbell Law Directory* to investigate their adversaries. But there's no reason you can't use it too. Because most law firms are listed in this directory, and because lawyers who furnish the information regarding their practice areas that is printed at the top of each entry, tend to be optimistic in naming these areas, the directory is not the best starting place for someone in search of a lawyer (unless you find that you need to hire a lawyer in another city). However, it is a very good place to gather information on lawyers; most of this information is self-evident from the entries in the directory. If you read a few *Martindale-Hubbell* listings carefully, you can gain some valuable insights into the qualifications of the lawyers on your list, such as:

- What law schools they attended—The differences in law school training diminish in importance in direct proportion to the number of years a lawyer has practiced, and, in any event, the good reputation of a school does not ensure that all its graduates are paragons of the legal profession. However, you should at least make sure that any lawyer you consider hiring graduated from an accredited law school, as opposed to one of the numerous unaccredited schools that still operate around the country. Ask a reference librarian to tell you whether a law school unfamiliar to you is accredited; you can probably also get this information by calling the administration office for the law school in question.

- Whether they were members of their law-school law review or moot court team—Law review membership and moot court experience are earmarks of smart, capable lawyers. Law students compete among themselves to earn a place on their schools' law reviews, which are respected legal journals written, edited, and published by students, or moot court teams, which are like debate teams that compete by trying fictitious lawsuits. A spot on either results in extra training in an important area. (This is not the case with some other law school extracurricular activities. You don't have to be Albert Einstein—or Learned Hand—to become, for example, president of the student bar association or of a law fraternity. And despite the fact that lawyers list such memberships in the *Martindale-Hubbell Law Directory* as if they indicated some accomplishment, any law student whose body is still warm can become a member of a law fraternity.)

- Where they worked previously—Judicial clerkships are like finishing school for young lawyers, and former judicial clerks are usually bright, precise, and serious, with high ethical standards. Similarly, a lawyer who once worked for the state attorney general or local district attorney's office or local federal prosecutor is likely to know the players and the terrain of the local civil judiciary system.

- Whether they have published scholarly articles—Although

most lawyers are technicians rather than scholars, it can't hurt to hire one who has earned the respect of his or her peers for expertise in some area, which is the chief result of publishing articles in law reviews or legal journals. Bear in mind, however, that a lawyer who has published articles on oil-and-gas law, for example, is unlikely to be interested in handling any trademark matter.

- Whether they are partners or associates in their firms—In every *Martindale-Hubbell Law Directory* entry for a law firm, the lawyers are listed in descending order of seniority and importance within the firm. The first lawyers listed are partners in the firm; they are called "members." In the directory, there is a horizontal line printed after the last of the partners' names that divides the sheep from the goats; any lawyer whose name is listed after this line is an associate attorney. Partners have more experience than associates, but associates charge smaller hourly fees than partners. Perhaps the best solution is to hire a junior partner or a senior associate; the names of such lawyers will be found hovering just above and below the line dividing the two classes of lawyers.

When you locate a copy of the *Martindale-Hubbell Law Directory*, plan to spend an hour researching the lawyers on your master list and make photocopies of the pages with their entries and those that reflect the names and addresses of their firms. Unless you can prevail upon a pal who is a lawyer to let you examine his or her firm's *Martindale-Hubbell* directory, you'll find a set of the volumes only in a library. That means that there will be a lawyer, a librarian, or paralegal around to explain how to use the directory and how to evaluate the information you find there. Ask questions. You're on a mission to perfect and protect your trademark, potentially one of the most valuable assets of your business, or to avoid being bested by the plaintiff who is suing you or the defendant you want to go after.

If you are conversant with Internet research or know someone who is, visit the Martindale-Hubbell Web site at *www.martindale. com*. You may look up lawyers by name and city to find those on your list of recommended lawyers. You can also search by practice area for your city. Since the online version of the directory will produce and display only fifty listings per search request, make your search request as narrow as possible. Instead of searching by practice area for lawyers who practice in the area of "intellectual-property law," which includes, among other areas, patent and copyright law as well as trademark law, choose the "other area" listing at the end of the list of practice areas. Then, in the box set aside for specifying the "other area," type "trademark." This should produce a more targeted search with reliable results.

A caveat about the *Martindale-Hubbell Law Directory*. Some of the best attorneys are the mavericks who practice alone or with only one or two partners precisely because they dislike the bottom-line mentality that rules the life of lawyers at many firms today. This may be especially true for trademark practitioners. Such sole practitioners and very small firms may not meet the criteria for listings in *Martindale-Hubbell*. Don't reject any lawyer who is recommended to you just because you can't find him or her listed in the *Martindale-Hubbell* directory. Instead, find out what you need to know in an expanded version of the next step in the process of finding a lawyer—the screening interview.

Employment Interviews

Clients often forget that their lawyers need them just as much as they need their lawyers. The practice of law is, after all, a way of earning a living. Almost any lawyer, given an appropriate case, will accept you as a client and be grateful for the fees your legal problem creates. This means that you should recognize your first meeting with each of the lawyers on your list of prospective lawyers for what it is, an employment interview. You won't be the only employer of the lawyer you hire, but you will be *an* employer of that attorney and should expect to be treated like the prospective source of revenue that you are.

The first thing to do is to call for an appointment with each of the lawyers on your master list of prospects. When you call, make sure that you mention two things to the people who answer the phone: (1) that you are a prospective client and (2) that you have been referred to the lawyer you are calling. These statements will get most of the lawyers you call to the phone. You can probably eliminate some of your prospective attorneys from consideration on the basis of these initial phone calls. If you like the sound of a lawyer during your first phone call to him or her, ask for a brief interview appointment. It may seem to you that it would be more efficient to interview the lawyers on your list by telephone, but you'll find out more about them and get a better feel for which one you want to hire if you visit their offices.

Any lawyer you call, or the lawyer's secretary, will tell you at the time you make the appointment whether there will be a charge for this initial consultation meeting. Don't interpret a fee for your first meeting as a sign that the lawyer who charges it is not for you. It is likely that any lawyer with whom you meet will give you some useful advice during the course of the meeting and, in any event, lawyers make money by selling their labor by the hour and some of the best of them charge for *every* hour they work. However, just as many good lawyers do not charge for initial meetings, regarding such meetings as a necessary predicate to a new client relationship rather than actual billable time.

Your screening interviews should be both short enough to be efficient and long enough to determine the answers to a few basic questions.

If you are involved in any conflict between two marks, it may be inevitable that your dispute will ripen into a lawsuit. Any lawyer who practices trademark law should be able to help you clear a new mark, file to register it, and use it properly. However, not all trademark lawyers have significant experience in trademark litigation, especially if they have been in practice only a few years. This means that you should hire a lawyer who has the ability to represent you in litigation or, at least, one who can call on the more extensive litigation experience of another lawyer in the same firm.

And although you should arm yourself for war, your goal should be a treaty; that is, you should try to settle any dispute on a satisfactory basis before it becomes a lawsuit. Litigation should be avoided because its costs so often outweigh its benefits, even for plaintiffs who prevail in court. To ensure that you will be able to achieve the results you want with as little expenditure of time and money as possible, you will want to hire an attorney who is open to the idea of settling your dispute without full-fledged litigation. Because litigators, like surgeons, often see the most extreme remedy available as the only one, you should also ask what success any lawyer you interview has had in settling disputes out of court, either by means of settlement agreements negotiated between lawyers or through some variety of alternative dispute resolution. Remember Ambrose Bierce's definition of litigation: "A machine which you go into as a pig and come out of as a sausage."

After you briefly describe the matter with which you need help, you should ask each lawyer you interview for a brief preliminary assessment of your chances of success. Pay attention to their answers; lawyers learn to make pretty reliable judgments even in on-the-spot evaluations. And remember that if a lawyer tells you that your mark is unregistrable or infringes another mark or that you are not likely to prevail in a dispute or lawsuit, he or she is obligated to give an honest opinion. You can do whatever you like with the information, but no lawyer can tailor an opinion just to tell you what you want to hear.

Besides what you can learn about a lawyer from the *Martindale-Hubbell* directory, there are several other indicators that you will be pleased with an attorney. Keep the following guidelines in mind when you interview the lawyers you consider hiring.

Remember that many of the best lawyers do not practice in big firms with luxurious offices in ritzy buildings. Before you are too impressed by a lawyer's fancy office, remember that it is the clients of that lawyer who pay for the oriental rugs and original art.

Remember, too, that the standards for membership in most bar associations are lenient; i.e., any lawyer who is licensed in the locality for which the bar association is organized and will pay the requisite dues can become a member. This means that a lawyer's memberships in his or her local, state, and national bar associations mean very little as far as establishing whether he or she is the better-than-average attorney you want to hire. Lots of the framed certificates indicating membership in organizations with fancy names that you may see in the offices of the lawyers you interview mean absolutely nothing to you as a consumer of legal services. However, certificates that indicate further training past law school or certification by some national association show, at least, a lawyer who is concerned with keeping current and developing the abilities necessary to adequately represent his or her clients.

Pay attention to the support staff you see in each lawyer's office. Past a point, it is immaterial to most people who need a lawyer's services whether the lawyer commands a platoon of secretaries, paralegals, and associates, since no client except a big corporation that needs mountains of paperwork churned out before next Wednesday is likely to need the services of all those other people. However, a good secretary, a skilled paralegal, or a sharp associate can make a client's life easier and diminish legal fees by making or returning phone calls that would otherwise be billed by the lawyer and handling—without charge in the case of a secretary and at a reduced rate in the case of a paralegal or associate—the more routine work performed for a client. Ask any lawyer you interview which other people in the firm would be working on your case and what their qualifications are. Try to meet these people before you terminate the interview. Give the lawyer points for friendly, intelligent subordinates who look and act like professionals.

Even if you are impressed with an attorney after your meeting, don't hire him or her on the spot. Most successful lawyers are skilled at selling themselves to prospective clients; an honest lawyer won't make promises he or she can't keep, but you should make allowances for the mild sales pitch any lawyer who is interested in your business will make, if for no other reason than that lawyer enthusiasm has been known to wane after a client has been "landed"— like a fish. This means that you should give yourself time to reflect on the substance of your meetings with the lawyers on your list and to compare your impressions of all of them and their evaluations of your trademark problem. The bigger the problem, the longer you should consider how to handle it and who should help you. Even if you like a particular lawyer, things may look different after you meet with the next one.

Give yourself at least a week for your round of interview meetings. Your time and money will be well spent. By the time your meetings are completed, you will have had the advantage of the preliminary opinions of several lawyers about the cost of the work you need help with or your chances of success in settling or winning your dispute, you will be considerably more educated about the issues involved, and you will have completed a crash course in Lawyers and Their Habitats.

When you make up your mind which lawyer you want to hire, call that lawyer to tell him or her that you want to engage his or her services. If you didn't like any of the lawyers you interviewed enough to hire one of them, repeat your research and start interviewing again. If any matter is too complicated for you to handle or settle on your own, it is important to get the right lawyer to help you, since the wrong one may be no help at all or even an impediment to your goals.

After you have hired a lawyer, you must know how to recognize common failings of lawyers to protect yourself against them. Regrettably, lawyers, as a class, are subject to most of the failings to which the rest of humankind is prey. Since lawyers are only human, you may never find one who doesn't displease you in some way. However, because lawyers *are* human, put up with your lawyer's foibles if his or her work is good and he or she seems truly concerned with your best interests. But don't tolerate any of the following serious faults, which are, at the least, indicators that the relationship is not working very well, and get another lawyer when you decide that any of the eight is a chronic problem.

The Eight Warning Signals of a Bad Lawyer

1. *Your lawyer does not return your phone calls promptly.*

Lawyers are like dentists; they are paid only for the work they perform. This means that your lawyer tries to turn every moment of the workday into billable time and that he or she probably really is "on the phone" or "in a meeting" or "in court" when you call. Moreover, as a time management technique, many lawyers never *take* telephone calls but, rather, return their calls only during the periods of the day they set aside for *making* calls. Don't be offended if you can't get your lawyer on the line every time you call. However, pay attention and complain if your lawyer does not get back to you promptly. "Promptly" usually means a return call the same day you call. It certainly means a return call within twenty-four hours. It also means that your lawyer's secretary will call to let you know that your lawyer is traveling or otherwise unavailable if he or she cannot call you back within twenty-four hours.

2. *Your lawyer fails to keep you informed.*

One of a lawyer's more important duties to his or her clients is to keep them well informed of the progress and status of the matters they entrust to him or her. Because lawyers are simply skilled agents who act on behalf of their clients only to the extent that those clients direct and authorize them to do so, the entire lawyer-client relationship is premised on the assumption that the client will be kept informed by the lawyer. This means that you should receive copies of any trademark searches conducted for you, any Trademark Office filings and correspondence, all your lawyer's substantive communications with your adversary's attorney, and any documents such as court filings, depositions, responses to interrogatories, etc., as well as an occasional phone call or update letter. No important transaction should occur without your prior knowledge and consent. This does not mean that your lawyer must check with you every time he or she picks up the phone or writes a letter, but, rather, that he or she should act only within mutually agreed parameters. If your lawyer seems to have forgotten that he or she works for *you*, complain about it. If he or she doesn't reform after your complaint, get another lawyer.

3. *Your lawyer fails to keep commitments.*

Every lawyer must reschedule a meeting or ask for an extension of a deadline occasionally, but there is no excuse short of being hospitalized or stuck in a blizzard that will suffice to explain away a lawyer's missing an important deadline or failing to show up for a meeting, deposition, or court appearance. Lawyers who miss deadlines and can't be relied on to show up when they say they will lose the respect of other lawyers and of judges, their credibility is damaged and, consequently, they may be less able to successfully negotiate on your behalf. You can lose important rights because of your lawyer's disinterest, disorganization, or overbooking. If your lawyer misses (as opposed to rescheduling) any important commitment without a really good reason, view him or her as an unexploded hand grenade; that is, get as far away from him or her as possible, as soon as possible, to avoid the injury that *will* result from his or her inability or unwillingness to handle your business carefully.

4. *Your lawyer fails to follow your instructions.*

The word "attorney" means, simply, "agent." Lawyers stand in the place of their clients and speak and act for them only to the extent that they are authorized to do so. Any lawyer who loses sight of this fact has ceased to act as an agent for her or his clients and has become, at least potentially, a loose cannon. Don't expect a lawyer who views you only as a vehicle for exercising his or her bag of professional tricks to change. Cut your losses and find an attorney who will take instruction.

However, don't view your lawyer's resistance to particular directives as mutiny. Lawyers are supposed to exercise their own informed judgment and any lawyer who blindly follows the orders of a client has abdicated a large part of a lawyer's professional duty. Expect that your lawyer will, in any given situation, enumerate for you the alternatives available to you, evaluate the wisdom of each of those alternatives, and make recommendations for action. The final decision in any such situation should be yours. You should expect that your lawyer will frankly tell you what is objectionable about any instruction that you give to which he or she objects, and you should know that any ethical lawyer will resign from representing you if you insist that he or she participate in any dishonest strategy. Watch out for a lawyer who doesn't object strongly to any suggestion that he or she stretch the truth or engage in any sort of monkey business. People seldom direct their dishonesty in only one direction; you may find that you are on the receiving end of your lawyer's lack of scruples if you expect or tolerate ethical corner-cutting from him or her.

5. *Your lawyer makes inflated or excessive claims regarding his or her abilities.*

As much as lawyers wish otherwise, no lawyer can really predict with certainty the outcome of any legal proceeding or negotiation. Regardless of how skilled your lawyer or how just your position, there are factors in any matter before the Trademark Office or in any trademark dispute over which neither you nor your lawyer has any control at all—the judgments of the Trademark Office or the attitudes and agenda of your adversary and of your adversary's attorney. No amount of skilled lawyering can persuade the Trademark Office to grant a registration when the trademark statute or the *Trademark Manual of Examining Procedure* dictates otherwise. And a really determined bad guy can derail even the most reasonable and competent attorney's strategies for a fair settlement of a dispute. If you are in court, the number of important factors out of your attorney's control increases. Among the things that are uncontrollable, there is no more unpredictable and unassailable factor than the judge who hears your case. Many judges are wise and fair and struggle to mete out the justice that they are supposed to dispense. Others make arbitrary and unfair rulings that are, seemingly, based more on what they had for breakfast than on any reasoned interpretation of the law.

All this is by way of saying that no lawyer can make reliable claims of success. During the course of a dispute or lawsuit, events can occur that no one can predict or control or mitigate; such events can defeat any lawyer. If you hear the words "I've never lost a suit," or "I've got that judge in my back pocket," or "This case is a cinch," issue from the mouth of your lawyer, pin him or her down before any such rash statement has evaporated. Your lines are "Is that so? It seems impossible that you've never lost a suit," and "What, exactly, makes you think you can persuade that judge to see things our way?" and "Really? If our winning is a foregone conclusion, then why didn't the defendant settle out of court?" Get another lawyer if you find that any large percentage of your lawyer's discussions embody such delusions of grandeur. One of the primary jobs of a lawyer is to communicate with precision. Your lawyer's routine overstatement of his or her abilities is likely to cause problems; at the least, such behavior makes him or her an unreliable advisor. Look for a sober, serious, careful lawyer instead. A serious lawyer may not be as entertaining, but he or she won't lead you down the garden path or out on a limb, either.

6. *Your lawyer is overly aggressive or hostile.*

Anyone who thinks that every good lawyer eats nails for breakfast should reconsider that assumption. Actually, there are very few lawyers for whom a consistent posture of aggression or hostility is effective for anything other than giving clients a false sense of security. As a practical matter, a lawyer who is always aggressive is not an effective representative for his or her clients. Lawyers should be fearless enough to ask for what their clients want, clever enough to figure out how to get it, and bold enough to engage in the occasional bluff. However, they also should keep in mind, *at all times*, the best interests of their clients. A lawyer who only knows how to fight and intimidate his or her adversaries is a hack who is lacking several of the tools a good lawyer knows how to use. The abilities to negotiate and strategize are at least as important to most lawyers as the ability to fight. Think about it. If your lawyer's actions only operate to activate the defenses of your adversary, it is much more likely that you will find yourself in a full-blown fight than able to make a reasonable settlement. Unless you want to spend your retirement fund paying the fees of an attorney who loves a good fight, expect your lawyer to control his or her temper and to expend his or her aggression in some manner other than useless sparring on your behalf.

7. *Your lawyer is less than frank in answering your questions.*

Sometimes lawyers, who are prone to get carried away on the wings of their own oratory, forget the value of plain statements of fact. This sort of tin-pot eloquence will never be eradicated completely from the repertoire of most lawyers, and it is unlikely in the extreme that it will vanish from the armory of litigators, many of whom are hams at heart. Further, some of your lawyer's windy explanations may be necessary to convey the information you request. Clients always think that *anything* can be explained briefly; in reality, a long, confusing explanation may really be the best answer possible to a question, even though the necessity for its length may not be apparent to the client.

However, you should pay attention if the answers you get from your lawyer are always too vague to satisfy your inquiries. If this long-windedness is chronic, ask your lawyer to respond to your questions more plainly and with more brevity. If he or she won't or can't change, consider whether the long-windedness is really intentional obfuscation. Long, complicated answers may be simply an occupational trait of lawyers, but mendacity should not be. Regardless of this, some lawyers do engage in various sorts of prevarication, ranging from hedging to outright lying, even with their clients, to whom they owe *at least* the truth. Any evasion of the truth by a lawyer in any statement to a client is the sign of an incompetent lawyer who is covering up his or her inadequacies or a lawyer who, like a cat with a mouse, is manipulating the client for selfish ends. Don't allow your lawyer to toy with you or the matter that you have entrusted to him or her. But don't discharge him or her until you have asked for an explanation of what you think is a lie. If your lawyer's explanation is not convincing, get another lawyer.

8. *Your lawyer overbills you.*

Because lawyers must make judgment calls at every turn in handling almost any client matter, it is often difficult to know when a lawyer is billing you for make-work. However, it is important to question your lawyer if you think you are being billed for unnecessary work, because an uncomplaining client who pays excessive bills without question can count on receiving more and bigger bills from his or her lawyer, who may view the client as a fatted calf.

No fee statement should come as a surprise to you. When you engage your lawyer's services, you should receive a letter or be asked to sign a short agreement that specifies your lawyer's hourly rate and billing policies. If the matter you entrust to your lawyer involves a trademark dispute or lawsuit and your lawyer agrees to work on a contingency-fee basis, you should receive a detailed fee agreement specifying: (1) what share of any award or settlement amount your lawyer will be entitled to; (2) what expenses you will be expected to pay; and (3) whether other expenses will come off the top of the judgment or settlement or will be deducted *from your share* of that amount.

Question any fee or expense you think is excessive. If your lawyer does not answer your questions frankly and to your satisfaction, don't pay the disputed amount until you are satisfied that the charge is fair, or offer to pay only what you believe is fair under the circumstances. Any lawyer with your interests at heart should be willing to explain any legitimate fee or billed expense that puzzles you and, within reason, to modify any billing practice to which you object.

Unless a lawyer has abandoned all pretense of living up to his or her professional and ethical standards, even a polite complaint letter or phone call from a client is likely to produce better behavior. In fact, any complaint except one about truly outrageous behavior should be polite and, to the extent possible, nonaccusatory. Despite occasional evidence otherwise, most lawyers will conduct themselves professionally if their clients make it obvious that they expect good treatment. The alternative, of course, is that a lawyer you reprimand, even mildly, will refuse to reform. If this happens and the transgression is substantive, find another lawyer. You get the behavior you put up with.

And then there are the sins of lawyers that require summary execution, without discussion, without possibility of a reduced sentence. It may be unlikely that any lawyer you investigate before hiring will ever commit any of these sins, all of which are major breaches of a lawyer's duty to his or her client. However, although lawyers don't like to admit that any such breaches ever occur, they sometimes do. In the burgeoning population of American lawyers, there are bound to be some who are truly corrupt, because of alcoholism or drug abuse or gambling, because of ineptitude, because of depression or some other mental illness, or because of simple, garden-variety venality. For lawyers, these mortal sins are failing to keep a client's secrets, stealing from a client, and lying to a client.

If at any time you find that your lawyer has committed any of these sins, terminate his or her services immediately by means of a hand-delivered letter in which you demand prompt delivery to you of your file and the return of any retainer or deposit against charges for legal work that has not yet been performed. Threats seldom produce the desired results and, if they are too rash, diminish the force of the threat, but you should include in your letter a measured statement that you will take your complaint to the lawyer-licensing board for your state if your lawyer fails to comply promptly with your demands. Then, if your lawyer's transgression was serious enough, or has caused you significant harm, file your complaint anyway. You will find that the lawyer-licensing board, which is a division of your state's supreme court, will take your complaint very seriously and that the only lawyer who will criticize your action is the one who will become the subject of the board's investigation.

Managing Your Lawyer

One important factor in obtaining satisfactory legal work that clients often overlook is that almost any lawyer's work will better satisfy his or her client if that person knows how to be a *good* client. Part of being a good client is technique and part is attitude.

Even a principled lawyer will represent you more satisfactorily if you know how to manage his or her work. There are several techniques that clients can employ to get the best services from their lawyers. Ordinarily, clients learn these lawyer management skills only after they have been through a few battles with the aid of several lawyers. Experience is a good teacher, but when it comes to figuring out how to manage lawyers, learning from experience is a bad method, because the information you need comes only after the fact and because your lawyer's meter is running while you learn. Fortunately, many techniques for managing a lawyer's work can be employed as easily and effectively by anyone who understands them as by an "experienced" client—a category you may, in any event, want to avoid.

Four of the most important lawyer management techniques are as follows:

1. *Give your lawyer the necessary information.*

Your lawyer needs accurate information in order to represent your interests. The first thing your lawyer will do is ask you a long list of questions. The more pertinent information you can give your lawyer, the less time he or she will have to spend ferreting out the information, and the smaller your fee bill will be. Try to give your lawyer complete information in an organized form as soon as it is requested. If you don't have the information your lawyer needs but can get it as easily as your lawyer can, gather it yourself to save yourself legal fees.

A corollary to the principle that your lawyer needs information in order to represent you is that he or she does not need a file cluttered with extraneous information. Points that you think are important may be, in actuality, beside the point. If your lawyer doesn't ask about some topics that you think are pertinent, ask whether the information will help. Save your tale to recount to your friends if your lawyer isn't interested, because the information you considered important is either immaterial, unreliable, inadmissible, or available in some better form elsewhere.

2. *Call your lawyer only when necessary.*

It is important to remember that the mere fact that the telephone on your desk is connected to the one in your lawyer's office doesn't mean that it is a good idea to call your lawyer every time you have a question or think of something he or she needs to know. Among other drawbacks, if you are paying your lawyer on an hourly basis, calling him or her every time you have the urge is likely to result in much higher legal fees. Most lawyers bill a minimum amount of time, usually a quarter hour, for any phone call and the time it takes to draft a file memo concerning the phone call. If your lawyer is working on a contingency-fee basis, too many calls from you will exasperate him or her, since he or she will not earn any more than the agreed-upon share of the settlement amount or judgment paid to you that he or she is already due for the extra work you create by calling too often.

One good technique for reducing time on the phone with your lawyer is to put your thoughts in a concise memo for your file. You don't have to hire a secretary or even learn to type to produce such memoranda—a legible handwritten memo will work. Even if your lawyer reads every word of your memo, less billable time will be consumed than if you furnish this information in the course of several phone calls.

Another good approach is to keep a running list of your thoughts and questions and look over and organize these notes before you call. Then, call your lawyer's secretary and make a phone appointment for fifteen minutes or half an hour in order to ensure that your lawyer will be waiting, with your file open, when you call. This saves endless games of telephone tag and won't create more fees than calling without an appointment. Of course, none of this applies to emergency calls, but in most trademark matters or disputes, there *are* very few true emergencies.

And remember that sometimes it is possible to address the questions you have to a lawyer's secretary or a paralegal or associate. These people are less difficult to get on the phone; if they can't answer your question, it may be possible for them to ask your lawyer the question you need answered and call you back with the answer.

3. *Don't quibble over ordinary charges.*

It is understandable and appropriate that clients get upset over unreasonable bills from their lawyers. If you receive a statement from your lawyer that you consider excessive, you *should* complain about it. In fact, it is far better for the long-term health of your relationship with your lawyer to question bills you don't understand than to allow them to go unchallenged. This does not mean, however, grilling your lawyer, or your lawyer's secretary, about every charge on your statement.

Part of the responsibility for ensuring that no part of your lawyer's statement comes as a surprise is yours. If your lawyer does not furnish you with a written description of his or her billing practices, including a list of the expenses incurred on your behalf that you will be expected to reimburse, ask for one so that you will know what to expect.

Expect to be asked for a retainer fee to cover the initial work that you hire your lawyer to perform and that you may be asked to make further occasional advance payments against fees and significant expenses. Expect to be charged a minimum of a quarter hour for any phone call made or taken by your lawyer on your behalf, including calls to and from you. Expect that all letters will be billed at a minimum of a half hour. Expect to be billed, at a reduced rate, for the services of paralegals. Expect to be billed for expenses incurred on your behalf, including postage, courier fees, long-distance telephone calls, photocopies, travel costs, trademark search fees, Trademark Office and court filing fees, and the costs of court reporters for depositions. In fact, at some firms, expect to be billed for all expenses that are even remotely attributable to work performed for you, including almost everything except the electricity consumed by the lights in your lawyer's office.

But, too, expect that your lawyer or his or her secretary will answer any questions you have about your bills and that, within reason, your objections will be taken seriously and your directions will be followed.

4. *Maintain the right attitude.*

Despite what many people may believe, most lawyers don't want passive clients. Such clients often make unrealistic demands on their lawyers, expecting them to pull rabbits out of hats, sometimes in situations where there are no good remedies for the clients' problems. Instead, lawyers want their clients to be, to a large extent, partners in the effort to reach the clients' goals or the search for solutions to the clients' problems. This means that you should take the attitude that the legal matter or problem belongs to you.

This sounds like a restatement of the obvious, but it really isn't. Once you stop thinking of the legal matter or problem you entrust to your lawyer as a matter that will, by necessity, be satisfactorily resolved by your lawyer simply because you have turned it over to him or her, and begin to view it as a matter that you may be able to accomplish or solve satisfactorily with the assistance of your lawyer, you will have a realistic view of your situation and will be less likely to be surprised by developments or disappointed by results. Your legal concern is *yours.* Your attorney can help you, but only because you hire him or her, furnish the necessary information and direction, and make the correct choices when the available options are presented to you.

♣

Use It Correctly or Lose It

T RADEMARKS, whether registered or not, can theoretically last perpetually. As long as someone markets goods or services under a name or symbol, it has a legal existence as a trademark. However, trademarks "die" every day.

Trademark Abandonment

One of the ways a trademark dies is by "abandonment"; that is, the owner of the mark ceases using it. This ordinarily happens to trademarks owned by underfinanced or unskilled marketers and to those that name unsuccessful products or services. Such abandonment is, of course, a result of a decision of the trademark owner. (Does Ford use EDSEL for *anything* anymore?) Sometimes a mark is abandoned because of some spectacularly bad event associated with it. The 1996 Valu-Jet air disaster in Florida may have resulted in the abandonment of the cartoon-plane logo that became familiar to people who had never before heard of the airline through weeks of news footage about the crash; Valu-Jet was sold and merged with another company soon afterward and the Valu-Jet name and logo fell into what will probably become permanent disuse. When a trademark really has been abandoned—that is, it has fallen out of use for a substantial period of time and its owner has no intent to revive it—it can be used by another marketer because it has ceased to represent the commercial reputation of the products of its original owner. (But remember that it is risky to adopt and use a mark that you believe to be abandoned without some investigation into the intentions of the original owner of the mark. Suspension of use of a mark may occur for several reasons other than the owner's intention to abandon it and, even if the owner does eventually abandon the mark, such intent cannot be deduced merely from a short period of disuse of the mark.)

Trademark Genericness

The second way trademarks die is almost the converse of the first situation, because such deaths often befall very famous trademarks and always occur against the will of the trademark owner. This form of trademark death results when a trademark becomes "generic," that is, when the word that formerly served as a trademark comes to signify to the general public the kind of product or service it names rather than representing a particular brand of that product or service. This form of trademark extinction should be of great interest to anyone who owns a trademark or participates in the marketing of the product or service it names. That is because loss of a trademark through its becoming generic is always a great financial loss to trademark owners, especially considering the fact that many trademarks become generic because they name extremely popular products or services; a mark that names a popular and successful product or service is a valuable mark indeed. Marketing people, graphic designers, and advertising creative people are the first line of defense against genericness.

"Escalator," "cellophane," "trampoline," "shredded wheat," "mimeograph," "linoleum," and "aspirin," all once named particular products of particular companies; they were trademarks rather than, as now, the generic terms for whole classes of goods. Because they became generic, that is, because they lost their status as the names

Once a trademark, not always a trademark.

They were once proud trademarks, now they're just names. They failed to take precautions that would have helped them have a long and prosperous life.

We need your help to stay out of there. Whenever you use our name, please use it as a proper adjective in conjunction with our products and services: e.g., Xerox copiers or Xerox financial services. And never as a

verb: "to Xerox" in place of "to copy," or as a noun: "Xeroxes" in place of "copies."

With your help and a precaution or two on our part, it's "Once the Xerox trademark, always the Xerox trademark."

Team Xerox. We document the world.

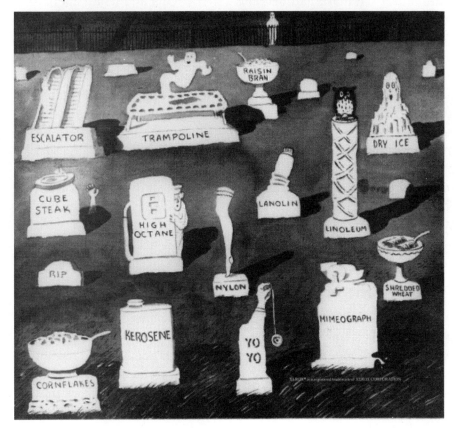

(Reprinted by permission of the Xerox Corporation.)

of particular products of particular companies, they can now be used by anyone.

In the case of the former trademark ESCALATOR, a court held that because consumers thought of all moving stairways as "escalators," ESCALATOR had lost its ability to point only to products of the Otis Elevator Company. In the decision that canceled Otis's fifty-year-old trademark registration for ESCALATOR, the court stated that the fact Otis itself had used its trademark in its own ads as "escalator," that is, as a generic term for a class of products, supported the contention that the mark had become generic. Otis and its ad agency goofed, and they paid the price by losing one of the company's most valuable assets, its famous trademark ESCALATOR.

Similar scenarios surrounded the ends of all the former trademarks mentioned above, and others. Ironically, it is the names of unique and innovative products that are most at risk of becoming generic. This is because the name of the first version of a groundbreaking product can come to mean that *type* of product in the minds of consumers, who may refer to all products of the same sort by the trademark of the first one they encountered. XEROX® is one trademark that is presently in danger of becoming a generic term (for photocopy machines and photocopies). LEVI'S®, FORMICA®, WALKMAN®, TUPPERWARE®, KLEENEX®, ROLLERBLADE®, and POST-IT® are similarly endangered.

Avoiding Genericness

In some cases, a company may be virtually powerless to prevent its trademark for a unique product that captures the public's imagination from falling into common usage as the name of the *type* of product rather than the name of one particular brand of that product. "Nylon," "yo-yo," and "zipper" may have been marks that no amount of care could have preserved from genericness. However, in almost every case a company can at least put up a fight to halt the fall of its marks into genericness, by care in its use of them and, when necessary, by ads that promote the names as trademarks.

A mark may become generic because consumers and the media begin to use it to refer to a class of products rather than to the products of one particular marketer, and it is important to take

When you use "Xerox" the way you use "aspirin," we get a headache.

X Boy, what a headache! And all because some of you may be using our name in a generic manner. Which could cause it to lose its trademark status the way the name "aspirin" did years ago. So when you do use our name, please use it as an adjective to identify our products and services, e.g., Xerox copiers. Never as a verb: "to Xerox" in place of "to copy", or as a noun: "Xeroxes" in place of "copies". Thank you. Now, could you excuse us, we've got to lie down for a few minutes.

THE
DOCUMENT
COMPANY
XEROX
Worldwide Sponsor

THE DOCUMENT COMPANY
XEROX

measures to squelch such incipient genericness. A bigger problem, however, is misuse of the trademark by its owner or those who use it under the owner's control, since such misuse can be a critical factor in a court's decision whether a mark has become generic, thereby losing its trademark significance.

The very least that is required of any trademark owner is that it police its own use of its trademark and the use of the mark by its licensees and agents, such as ad agencies and retailers. Proper use of a company's trademark can have very real dollars-and-cents consequences for the trademark owner. Trademarks are often considered to be among the most valuable assets of the companies that own them because they often represent a certain steady share of the market for the products they name. If a trademark becomes generic (and therefore available for use by anyone), that market identity and share are lost.

Proper trademark usage, crucial for protecting the exclusive ownership of a trademark, involves a few rules of "trademark grammar" that all marketing people should know and use. Remember that:

- A trademark is always an adjective, never a noun. It is "CHEER® laundry detergent," never simply "CHEER"; hence "Get your clothes clean with CHEER® laundry detergent." Think of "CAMPBELL'S® soups," "TOTES® umbrellas," "HOLIDAY INN® hotels," and "POLAROID® film."

- A trademark is a proper adjective. It is "ROLLERBLADE® in-line skates," never "I want some ROLLERBLADES." Think of "LEVI'S® jeans," "EGG MCMUFFIN® breakfast sandwiches," and "CHANEL® perfumes."

- A trademark is always singular, never plural. It is "EASY SPIRIT® shoes," never simply "EASY SPIRITS." Think of CRAYOLA® crayons," "APPLE® computers," and "KLEENEX® tissues."

- Trademark variations should be avoided. Trademarks should never be made possessive, i.e., it is never "HEINZ's great taste" but is, rather, "The great taste of HEINZ 57® steak sauce." And if the mark is registered or ordinarily used in one typeface or format, don't change its customary appearance without careful thought; otherwise, how will consumers recognize their old friend? Similarly, avoid changes in the verbal content of the mark at all costs; it is "Fried to a golden brown with CRISCO® all-vegetable shortening!" not "CRISCO-ed to perfection again!"

Although these rules aren't really that difficult to remember or follow, not all trademark owners follow them religiously—maybe because they are uninformed or careless or because they think their marks are so famous they can ignore the rules. You, however, should tend to your own mark carefully, in the hope and expectation that someday it will become famous enough that you can hire a dozen or so trademark lawyers to tend it for you.

The problem may not be remembering or following the rules in using your valuable trademark, but whether *others* do. If you own a trademark or are in a job that requires you to create or approve ads, packaging, signage, press releases, or other materials that embody a trademark, you owe a duty to yourself or to your employer or client to see that the mark is used correctly. There are several ways to do this.

Following the Rules

One of the best ways to avoid trademark genericness is to produce a set of trademark usage guidelines for your company. These guidelines can educate anyone who writes or produces any advertising or public relations materials for you in the proper use of trademarks in general and your mark in particular. It can also be furnished to journalists who write about your product or your company and can be made a part of any agreement to license your trademark to another company (see the discussion on trademark licensing below). Your trademark usage guidelines should include a section on graphic standards for the use of anyone who reproduces your mark in any but purely verbal forms. This section should specify colors and typefaces and should give examples of the proper visual forms of your mark.

You can even get creative with these guidelines and print them on t-shirts that you use as trade-show giveaways, style sheets that you furnish to the media, and posters for your retailers. The main thing is to get the word out to anyone who has or may have any reason to use your mark in or on anything the public sees.

Another good method for ensuring proper use of your trademark by your company and its agents and licensees is to appoint a trademark czar to review and approve any materials that embody your trademark before they are produced and duplicated. Anyone given this responsibility should be really capable of understanding and carrying out the job. This is not a task that can be delegated to a file clerk who doesn't have enough to do; your trademark enforcer should be a lawyer or senior marketing person who thoroughly understands trademark law and the purposes of correct trademark usage as well as the consequences of incorrect usage. Establish a formal system for review of anything besides internal documents and be consistent in enforcing the rules of usage that you have decreed apply to your mark. Treat the person who is charged with protecting your trademark with at least as much respect as you give your chief financial officer; if you have a hit product on your hands, the trademark that names it will be well worth the attention.

Fending Off Infringers

The law imposes upon trademark owners the obligation to police their trademarks. That is, the quid pro quo for the protection the law gives your commercial reputation is the obligation to protect that reputation from those who would damage it and to take action to ensure that the mark continues to point to *one* source for the goods or services it names. The trademark owner's interests are concurrent with those of consumers: if the trademark remains strong and distinctive, it will become more valuable and consumers may continue to rely on the mark as an indicator of a quality product.

Policing a trademark means keeping an eye out for marks that are similar to your mark and acting quickly to stop the use of any that you think infringe it. There are lots of ways to do this, and many degrees of vigilance. Most trademark owners watch the trade publications for their industry; consciously or unconsciously, one of their reasons for doing so is to discover whether any marketer of a similar product or service is using a name or symbol similar to their own trademarks. If they discover such uses, they will immediately take action, usually by calling their lawyers. All this is obvious. Any businessperson needs to keep up with what is going on in his or her area of commerce and most businesspeople know that a mark that is too similar to their own can present big problems, even if they don't know that what they would be complaining about is trademark infringement.

Finding out about less direct conflicts may be more difficult. Large corporations use in-house paralegals and employ "watching services" to discover the use of any marks that may conflict with their marks. These trademark owners review trade publications, of course, but they also carefully watch the weekly *Trademark Official Gazette,* which is available by subscription from the U.S. Government Printing Office. Typically, corporations will challenge marks that are published for opposition if they seem to be too close to those the corporations own. Sometimes big companies challenge marks that are *not* really similar to their own marks by filing or threatening to file opposition proceedings in an effort to halt the granting of registration for the new marks. Many such disputes, especially those involving marks that are not really threats to an established mark, are settled by mutual agreement before the opposition proceedings are actually commenced. The trademark owner's idea, in such a circumstance, may be to be able to demonstrate that it acts promptly to stop any threat to its established mark. Courts look at such evidence in evaluating whether a trademark owner has a history of protecting its mark from infringers.

Nevertheless, it must be said that nothing in the law requires a trademark owner to rush to the courthouse to file a trademark-infringement suit every time there is a question of infringement. There are effective methods for settling trademark-infringement disputes besides slugging it out in court. And quite often trademark owners may be unsure whether the actions of another marketer really do constitute infringement; for example, does the name of its software program infringe your registered mark for an LSAT review course? However, if you "sleep on your rights" long enough and fail to challenge an infringer, a court hearing your tardy trademark-infringement suit may rule that your previous failure to object to the actions of the defendant you are suing for infringement has allowed that defendant to depend on your apparent acquiescence to its use of the suspect mark and that to enjoin that use now would be unfair.

All this means that there are two rules for policing trademarks.

The first rule is "Rust never sleeps"; that is, vigilance against trademark infringers must be ceaseless and tireless to be effective— you must know what is going on in the marketplace, which is both the birthplace and the stomping ground for trademarks, which do not exist at all if they do not exist there. The second rule is "Walk softly, but carry a big stick"; that is, don't file a trademark-infringement suit until you are sure of your facts, have tried to settle the dispute satisfactorily out of court, and have sought competent advice about the probable outcome of your suit, but be ready to act decisively if you determine that you *must* sue to stop the erosion of your rights.

Although it is important from the inception of your trademark to use it correctly and to see that others do so, the more famous it becomes and the more successful the product it names, the more vigilance it deserves. A viable trademark, that is, a memorable mark that is capable of federal registration, is like a small savings account. If you tend it carefully, it will grow in value. This means that you should watch out for marks that are similar to your fledgling mark and act quickly to stop the use of any that you think infringe it. And if someone uses your mark in a way that could contribute to its becoming generic, take a cue from the owners of the most valuable trademarks and write a letter asking that person to reform—it can be a nice letter, but it needs to be firm and to give specific examples of correct use of your mark. Let them know that you are watching.

To find out more about trademarks and how to protect and manage them, call the International Trademark Association (INTA) at 212/768-9887. The INTA, an association of (mostly corporate) trademark owners, publishes a number of reliable publications that are useful to trademark owners, among them handbooks on trademark searching and trademark administration, which is the management and protection of a trademark. Many are written for marketing people and other business executives rather than for lawyers. Annual dues for the organization are, at $850, hefty for any but prosperous trademark owners, but many of its programs, such as seminars on trademark law and trademark issues, and publications are available to nonmembers. Ask the INTA to send you information about the association and a list of its publications.

Trademark Licensing and Its Pitfalls

One of the best ways to exploit and profit from a trademark is to license it to someone else who wants to use it to sell toy bears or auto parts or hotel services. Since you, as the trademark owner, are paid for the use of your trademark and do not put up the money to manufacture the products or provide the services that you license to be offered in conjunction with your mark, trademark licensing can literally create income from thin air for you. It can also result in your killing the goose that laid the golden egg, since allowing anyone to use your trademark whose use of it, for whatever reason, is not controlled by you will result in your loss of your mark.

Being asked to license your trademark is exciting. It means, among other things, that your mark has become famous enough to attract the attention of consumers and that it stands for a quality product that consumers desire. But licensing your trademark means letting someone else use it, and unless you control that use, you have no way to ensure that your licensee is maintaining the good reputation that your trademark represents. The law views your allowing someone else to use your mark without your controlling that use in much the same way it views your acquiescing to use of your mark by infringers who use it *without* your permission. In either case, your mark has ceased to point to one source—you—for the goods or services it names.

Whenever anyone approaches you with a proposal to license your trademark, the first thing you should do after hearing the proposal is to call your trademark lawyer. You can probably create a mark yourself, clear it for use, at least preliminarily, figure out how to use it properly, and, maybe, register it—without the help of a lawyer. This is not the case with trademark licensing.

At the very least, a trademark license must be documented in a written agreement. Any attempt at verbal licensing would be viewed by a court as merely "naked licensing," that is, as your having granted permission to someone else to use your trademark without any real effort to control that use. And it may be nearly impossible to determine later just what the terms of any agreement are when they have not been memorialized in writing.

And your written trademark-licensing agreement must include

some very specific language in order to suffice to control the use of your mark. In fact, the word "license" means a permission granted by one person, the "licensor," who owns a right, to another person, the "licensee," who is permitted to exercise some of the rights of the licensor. At a minimum, a trademark-licensing agreement should include provisions governing the following important points of agreement:

- the grant of license—this provision is the heart of a trademark-licensing agreement. It specifies by whom and to whom the right to use the trademark is granted and typically conditions the grant upon the licensee's compliance with the other terms of the agreement. Further, most good licensing agreements provide that if the grant of license is not exercised, that is, if the licensee fails to actually use the trademark in the whole territory and throughout the entire term of the agreement, the agreement may be terminated by the licensor. This serves to free up the valuable trademark for licensing to another company if the licensee fails to exploit it as agreed; in other words, a licensee must "use it or lose it."

- the territory—this provision specifies in which states or countries the licensee is permitted to use the trademark. You may, for instance, license one company to use your mark in the eastern United States, and another in the western United States.

- the term—this provision specifies the start and finish dates for the licensee's use of the trademark. As with the territory provision, and just as occupying a rental property past the expiration of a lease is trespassing, any use outside the period specified in the licensing agreement is trademark infringement.

- the product (or services) licensed—this provision is also very important. It specifies the exact products or services that the licensee may market under the licensed mark. The more carefully drafted the trademark-licensing agreement, the more specific this provision. In other words, a good agreement will specify that the licensed mark may be used in conjunction with "boys' red, blue, yellow, and purple two-eyelet, rubber-soled canvas play shoes, up to size 8, manufactured in accordance with the specifications set out in Exhibit C, attached hereto and made a part of this agreement by this reference."

- quality specifications for the licensed product (or services)—one of the ways the licensor controls use of its mark is to agree that the mark may be applied only to products or services of satisfactory quality. This protects the standing of the licensed trademark and the licensor's investment in it, since just as the good reputation of the product or services to which the mark was first applied will reflect favorably on the licensed product or services, an inferior licensed product would reflect badly on the well-regarded trademark and product. These quite detailed specifications are typically written separately and attached to the licensing agreement as an exhibit, that is, on an attached sheet that is specifically agreed to be part of the agreement.

- quality control—a trademark licensor must be able to determine whether the licensee is living up to the quality specifications for the licensed product in order to protect the licensed mark. All proper trademark-licensing agreements contain a provision allowing the licensor, or the licensor's representatives, access to the manufacturing facilities of the licensee in order to ascertain whether the licensed product or service is and continues to meet those quality specifications.

- trademark usage—the actions of a trademark licensee with regard to the way the licensed mark is used accrue to the benefit or detriment of the licensor. This means that the licensor must specify the manner in which the mark is to be used on the product (or in advertising services) and on or in packaging, signage, advertising, etc. Again, such provisions for use of the trademark often appear in an attachment to the basic agreement; this is one very good use for the trademark usage guidelines that trademark owners write for their own use and that of their agents and retailers.

- termination provisions—all good trademark-licensing agreements give the licensor the right to terminate the agreement if the licensee breaches any of the provisions of the agreement. Typically, small or accidental breaches may be "cured" within a specified short period and the agreement will continue if the licensor is satisfied that the complained-of actions or conditions have been remedied. In the event of really significant and intentional breaches of the agreement (such as using the licensed mark outside the agreed territory), the licensor usually may, at its option, immediately terminate the agreement.

- payment of royalties—this is, of course, another of the most important provisions of any trademark-licensing agreement. Typically, the owner of the licensed trademark is paid an agreed fee per unit of the product that is sold in conjunction with the mark. For services, payment is usually a set fee paid periodically during the term of the agreement. Many agreements provide that if the licensee fails to make to the licensor more than one such payment, the licensor may immediately terminate the agreement.

The best way to proceed with any proposed licensing is to ask the would-be licensee to state the basic terms of the offered agreement (term, products licensed, territory, royalty, etc.) in a letter to you. Before you respond, take the letter to your lawyer and ask for advice concerning the fairness of the terms of the agreement. In addition, get some information about the would-be licensee; it's a lot easier to work with a solvent company that can do what it says it can than to find yourself one of the creditors of an insolvent company. Ask for references from other companies that have licensed their marks to the company that wants to license yours. And make sure that your lawyer writes the licensing agreement or, at least, that the first-draft contract offered to you by your licensee is thoroughly negotiated by your lawyer. There's a big difference between *your* paper and *theirs*—it's often much easier to get the deal you want when you start from a contract your lawyer drafted for you.

Condemned to Anonymity

The following terms were held by the Trademark Office or a court to be incapable of serving as indicators of particular sources for the goods and services they named because they had become, in the minds of consumers, generic terms for those products or services. After being declared to be nontrademarks, these terms became free for anyone to use in describing products or services and ceased to be the exclusive property of their originators.

AL-KOL for rubbing alcohol
ASPIRIN for acetyl salicylic acid
BABY OIL for mineral oil
BATH OIL BEADS for bath oil, water softener, and perfume
BODY SOAP for body shampoo
BRASSIERE for women's bras
BUNDT for a type of ring coffee cake
CELLOPHANE for transparent cellulose sheets
COLA for a soft drink
COMPUTER LEARNING CENTER for computer courses
THE COMPUTER STORE for retail computer sales services
CONSUMER ELECTRONICS MONTHLY for a magazine for electronics
    enthusiasts
COPPERCLAD for copper-coated conductors
CUBE STEAK for tenderized steaks
DRY ICE for carbon dioxide in solid form
EASTER BASKET for an Easter floral basket
ESCALATOR for moving stairways
EXPORT SODA for an exported soda cracker
FLOR-TILE for wooden flooring
FLOWERS BY WIRE for intercity floral delivery services
FLUID ENERGY for hydraulic/pneumatic equipment
HAIR COLOR BATH for a hair-coloring preparation
HARD TO FIND TOOLS for a tool mail-order service
HOAGIE for sandwiches
HONEY BAKED HAM for honey-glazed hams
JUJUBES for gum candies
LIGHT BEER for a light-bodied beer
METALOCK for a metal repair method
MONOPOLY for a real estate–trading board game
MONTESSORI for an education method and associated toys
MULTISTATE BAR EXAMINATION for a bar examination given in several
    states
MURPHEY BED for beds that fold into a wall or closet for storage
THE PILL for oral contraceptives

POCKET BOOK for paperback books
PRIMAL THERAPY for a type of psychotherapy
PROM for programmable read-only memory computer systems.
RUBBER ROPE for an elasticized rubber rope product
SAFE T PLUG for electrical plugs
SHREDDED WHEAT for baked wheat biscuits
SOCIOGRAPHICS for a technique of management consulting
SOFTSOAP for liquid hand soap
SUPER GLUE for rapid-setting cyanoacrylate adhesives
SURGICENTER for a surgical center
THERMOS for vacuum-insulated bottles
TRAMPOLINE for rebound tumbling equipment
VIDEO BUYERS GUIDE for a magazine for videotape buyers
WORK WEAR for industrial clothing
YO-YO for return tops

❖

CHAPTER 8

Other People's Trademarks

LMOST EVERYONE KNOWS that selling toothpaste or sneakers or brokerage services by using a trademark that belongs to someone else is a quick ticket to a federal suit for trademark infringement. The law allows marketers to protect themselves from interlopers who want a free ride on their commercial coattails; they do this by means of lawsuits to preserve the integrity of their trademarks, which represent them to the public. The penumbra of protection granted an established trademark extends to identical marks and to marks which, although not identical, are similar enough to confuse consumers. Usually, the comparison to determine trademark infringement is made between marks used to market similar products or services. However, the more famous and unusual the trademark, the wider the scope of protection trademark law grants it; no one can use KLEENEX® or COCA-COLA® or EXXON® for *any* product without encountering serious opposition from platoons of trademark lawyers for those companies, especially since the Trademark Dilution Act became effective in early 1996. (See chapter 5 for a more detailed explanation of the Trademark Dilution Act.)

There are other ways to infringe a trademark besides adopting a name for a product or service that is confusingly similar to an established mark for a similar product or service. Because trademark owners are vigilant in protecting their trademarks, wariness in the matter of other people's trademarks is a very good idea. However, such wariness can lead to an exaggerated fear of trademarks that belong to others and unnecessary maneuvering to avoid any mention or depiction of them. Surprisingly enough, there are some circumstances when using someone else's trademark *is* safe.

Broadly speaking, the law gives a trademark owner protection against any action that creates confusion about that trademark in the minds of consumers. This means that the dividing line between safe and unsafe uses of a trademark is where consumer confusion begins. Determining whether a given use of someone else's trademark will lead to a lawsuit is simply a matter of determining, under all the circumstances, whether that use will confuse anyone.

There are two common varieties of use of someone else's trademark that are usually safe and one that is, by definition, almost never safe. An examination of each of these situations will demonstrate the considerations involved in using other people's trademarks.

Incidental Use of Trademarks

More than one creative director has called in a lawyer to evaluate whether the presence of a COKE® can sitting on a table in a photograph is enough to disqualify the photo for use in an ad that isn't supposed to advertise COKE products. Before the lawyer can answer the question, he or she will have to see the photograph in question and read the ad copy, because the two important factors in evaluating whether the Coca-Cola Company is likely to sue are the emphasis of the photograph and the context of the use of the COKE logo.

Trademarks are a part of our world; they so pervade every environment of modern life that it is next to impossible to walk down a street or visit a public place or sit in a room without being surrounded by trademarks of every sort. This means that any realistic depiction of a street scene or restaurant setting or home or office situation will include representations of the trademarks found in that environment. Even though the trademarks that appear in such depictions are the valuable property of the companies that own them, in a way they also belong to the rest of us because they are a part of our lives. The First Amendment protects commercial speech such as advertising as well as other sorts of speech. This means that, as a matter of free speech, we have a right to "mention" the trademarks around us, either verbally or visually.

Which brings us back to the COKE® can in that photograph. Although free speech gives us the right to talk about or depict the world we live in, including trademarks, trademark law limits that right to some extent by discouraging certain sorts of uses of trademarks. The law would allow the Coca-Cola Company to sue the ad agency and the agency's client for trademark infringement if anything about the photo that included the COKE can implied that there was some connection between COCA-COLA® and the product advertised in the ad for which the photo was used. The same would be true if consumers could infer from the ad that the Coca-Cola Company somehow sponsored the ad or the product it advertised. As a practical matter, it is not likely that either of these grounds for suit would exist unless the COKE logo was legible and the can on which it appeared was a prominent element of the photograph; a background depiction of the can wouldn't create a problem, especially if the can wasn't an emphasis of the photograph.

Similarly, the context of the appearance in an ad of a "borrowed" trademark is important. If the COKE can photograph depicted the scene around the pool at an upscale resort hotel in an ad for that hotel, implying, however obliquely, that COCA-COLA is a favorite drink of carefree, wealthy people who look good in stylish bathing suits, the Coca-Cola Company probably would not object to the incidental appearance of its name and logo in the ad. If, however, the COKE can appeared in an objectionable photograph or if that photograph were used in any unsavory context, the Coca-Cola Company would be inclined to take whatever action was necessary to halt further use of the photo, especially if the COKE can was prominent in the photograph. The Coca-Cola Company, along with everybody else in the world, knows that villains and heroes and every other variety of human being drink CocA-CoLA soft drinks. However, it is understandable that no one in Atlanta except the lawyers who earn their keep by guarding the various valuable CocA-CoLA trademarks would like to see an ad photo prominently depicting a COKE can lying on a heap of rancid garbage or a broken COKE bottle being wielded as a weapon in a bar fight. Similarly, an identifiable depiction of a CocA-CoLA product used in an ad for a topless bar or cigarettes or a personal hygiene product could earn the animosity of the Coca-Cola Company. Any use of a trademark in an unsavory context can lead to a claim of product disparagement, which is comparable to a defamation suit brought on behalf of a trademark.

Comparative Advertising

Strangely enough, there is one variety of calculated, obvious use of other people's trademarks that will seldom cause trouble if carried out carefully. This is the use of trademarks belonging to competitor companies in comparative advertising. Trademark law does not prohibit *non*trademark or informational uses of the trademarks of others but, rather, punishes uses that confuse consumers. Comparative advertising informs consumers by explicitly comparing the merits of one product with those of another. The competitor's product, which always suffers from the comparison, is mentioned specifically in the ad copy and its package is usually pictured beside the advertiser's product in a head-on shot. Such ads require by their very nature that the products compared be carefully identified before the distinctions between them are drawn; only a very clumsy ad would fail to make entirely clear whether JOY® detergent or IVORY® detergent cut grease faster in laboratory tests. The test for trademark infringement is whether the public will be confused by the use of the mark. Since the possibility of consumer confusion is eliminated in comparative advertising, so is the likelihood of any charge of trademark infringement.

However, only claims that are truthful and that can be substantiated are safe. Because exaggerated claims or claims that can't be documented can lead to false advertising suits or unfair competition claims, every statement in a comparative advertising campaign should be carefully documented and every element of the campaign should be carefully designed.

Comparative advertisements can safely make use of competitors' trademarks if they are carefully constructed. Using a photo of another company's product or mentioning the product by name in an ad that compares it to your company's product is not an infringement of the trademark rights of the other company if the ad truthfully compares the products named by the trademarks and if the character and arrangement of the visual elements and the content of the ad copy do not create any likelihood that consumers will somehow mistakenly believe that your company's product has some relation to the product of the other company.

Although properly designed comparative advertising does not usually lead to trademark-infringement suits, there is one caveat. Whenever you use a trademark belonging to someone else in an ad, it is only prudent to state who owns that trademark in order to emphasize that the mark has no connection with the advertiser's product. This is easily accomplished by means of a "footnote" ownership statement. That is, a short statement should be included somewhere along the bottom margin or up the side margin of print ads and at the bottom of the screen in television commercials to the effect that "DOVE® is a registered trademark of the Lever Brothers Company."

The competitor's trademark should be used in exactly the form it appears on the competitor's product; that is, if it is a federally registered trademark and bears the ® symbol, that symbol should be used in the ownership statement. If the mark is not registered, no such symbol will appear, or the ™ symbol will be used in conjunction with the mark. In this event, the usage as it appears on the product should be duplicated and the ownership statement should read something like this: "CRUNCHIES™ is a trademark of the Toasted Oats Company and is not owned or licensed by the makers of SWEETIES™ brand cereal." A statement that your client's competitor owns its mark should completely eliminate any valid claim that the comparative ad creates confusion regarding the ownership of the mark or the manufacturer of the product it names. However, because not just any such disclaimer will suffice, any such ad and proposed disclaimer should be reviewed, before the ad is published, by a trademark lawyer, who can evaluate the possibility that the ad will result in an infringement lawsuit.

It is important to remember that the laws regarding comparative advertising in other countries may vary considerably from those in the United States. Be especially sure that any ad you prepare that mentions another company's trademark and will be published or circulated outside the United States will not furnish the owner of the other trademark with grounds for suit. Marketers use comparative advertising because it is effective—a comparative ad can lure consumers away from a product they are in the habit of buying on the strength of its convincing claims of the benefits of a rival product that is "new and improved" or simply "more effective in 75 percent of laboratory tests." This is enough to make the owners of the product that fares badly in such comparisons want to do whatever they can to stop the further publication of the ad. A lawsuit can do this. If a competitor finds your comparative advertising objectionable and the law in one or more of the countries where the ad appears supports that viewpoint, you will be vulnerable in any country where your competitor can, with a straight face, file a suit. Maybe U.S. law, with its predisposition to allow free speech in all possible contexts, can't be used as a club to stop your trumpeting the better performance of your product, but the laws of other markets may, and every segment of international commerce counts. Japanese or Swedish or German money can fatten the bottom line for marketers just as well as American dollars, and perhaps somebody who works for your competitor wouldn't mind a long trip abroad at company expense to hire and supervise the lawyers who will be suing you under laws that you never heard of. Since you can't keep a tame trademark lawyer in your desk drawer to consult whenever you need advice, put his or her phone number on your ROLODEX® rotary card file (this is an example of correct usage of a trademark) *and* on your speed dial.

Trademark Parody

When a company decides to market a product under a name that is a parody of another mark, it is engaging in trademark parody. Trademark parody is almost always a bad idea, for two reasons. The first reason is that one of the kinds of confusion that trademark owners can legitimately complain about in court is "dilution," which is a claim that someone's use of an established mark is eroding the mark's strength even though the complained-of use is made in connection with a product that is unrelated to the product named by the established mark. If this fact alone isn't enough to convince you that trademark parody is almost invariably a dumb idea, consider this: only very famous trademarks are parodied—a parody of an obscure mark just wouldn't work. This means that the parodist is picking on a company rich enough to finance a trademark-infringement lawsuit out of its petty cash. And since the passage of the Trademark Dilution Act, suits for dilution are easier for owners of famous marks to file and win. (The Federal Express suit to stop the use of FEDERAL ESPRESSO for a coffeehouse is a good example of a parody use of a famous trademark that ran afoul of the Trademark Dilution Act's proscriptions.)

Another factor in trademark parody that often contributes to the problems that parodists face is that the parodied mark is often the butt of a joke, which may be an off-color joke. Nobody likes wise guys. The owners of the parodied mark may be so enraged by the parody of their mark that they will rush to file a trademark-infringement suit and ask for an injunction against the parodist. Courts are usually sympathetic to the interests of the owners of famous trademarks; as a result, trademark parodists are routinely enjoined from pursuing their bad jokes at the expense of the well-known marks they parody.

You can understand trademark parody better by considering a few trademark parody cases in which the parodists were ordered by the court to give up making jokes at the expense of the plaintiff trademark owners. The pairs of marks that were the subjects of these suits tell the story in themselves; if reading the list makes you wince, you're getting the right idea about trademark parody. Not surprisingly, all these defendants lost in court.

PLAINTIFF COMPANY	DEFENDANT TRADEMARK
Coca-Cola Company	"ENJOY COCAINE" (used, on a poster, in a script and color identical to those used for the COCA-COLA® logo)

Anheuser-Busch, Inc.	"WHERE THERE'S LIFE . . .THERE'S BUGS" (for combination floor wax-insecticide, in a parody of the Anheuser-Busch slogan "WHERE THERE'S LIFE . . . THERE'S BUD")
General Electric Company	"GENITAL ELECTRIC" (used, on men's underwear, in a script monogram similar to the GENERAL ELECTRIC® script logo)
Johnny Carson	"HERE'S JOHNNY" (used, as the name of a line of portable toilets, in a parody of the phrase associated with the famous comedian; no trademark infringement was found, but the court found that Mr. Carson's right of publicity had been violated)

Not every trademark parody is ruled a trademark infringement. For example, the use in a florist's ad campaign of the slogan "THIS BUD'S FOR YOU" was held not to infringe the trademark rights of Anheuser-Busch, Inc. In its ruling, the court specifically mentioned the innocuous and pleasant nature of the florist's slogan. As a practical matter, all this tells us is that *sometimes* parodists win in court. Since paying to defend a lawsuit is almost as much a misfortune as losing it, this is really no encouragement to would-be parodists. The best thing to do with famous trademarks is to steer clear of them, especially if your parody is smutty or would associate a famous mark with an unsavory product.

More than one trademark-infringement lawsuit has been brought simply because the trademark owner was angry and felt like doing something about it. If this doesn't scare you, consider the fact that owners of famous trademarks have whole platoons of trademark lawyers who have to justify their existence by periodically going after evildoers. If they are short of true malefactors this month, you and your ad may look like very good targets. When it comes to using someone else's famous trademark in an ad without permission, discretion really is the better part of valor.

The Etiquette of Trademark Usage

The only thing left to say about using other people's trademarks is that you should do so carefully. This boils down to the following four rules:

1. Trademarks are proper adjectives; remember to use them as such. It is a "Kleenex® tissue," not just a "kleenex," and you wear "Levi's® jeans," not just "levis."

2. Trademarks should never be used as nouns or verbs; you do not "Xerox®" a document, you make a photocopy of it, and it *is* a "photocopy," not simply a "xerox."

3. Spell it right. Most importantly, capitalize trademarks; it is "Coke®," not "coke," and "Cuisinart®," not "cuisinart."

4. Give a mark its due. If it is a registered mark, use the ® symbol in conjunction with the mark in at least the two or three most prominent uses of the mark in a text or an ad. If it is not registered, use informal trademark notice, i.e., the ™ superscript or subscript, if the owner of the mark does so on its products. (If the mark names a service, the trademark owner may use ℠ to indicate this.)

If you are confused about the proper spelling of a trademark or whether it is federally registered and therefore entitled to be escorted by the ® symbol whenever it appears in print, you can research the mark on the International Trademark Association (INTA) Trademark Checklist Web site at *www.inta.org/tmchklst.htm*. This Web site lists nearly four thousand trademarks and the generic terms for the products and services they name and indicates proper spelling, capitalization, and punctuation. If you can't find the mark you are investigating or don't have access to the Internet, call the INTA Trademark Hotline at 212/768-9886; the hotline operates weekdays from 2:00 P.M. to 5:00 P.M. eastern standard time.

Your rights won't be affected if you fail to follow these rules in using other people's trademarks, but theirs may be diminished. A trademark that is used incorrectly can become "generic"; that is, the mark loses its ability to refer to a particular product or service and comes to indicate a whole class of products. If this happens, the original owner of the mark loses the exclusive right to use it. This happened to "aspirin," and "escalator," and "thermos." In determining whether a mark has lost its significance as an indicator of *one* company's products or services, courts often consider whether a trademark owner has acted against infringers. You may have no legal *duty* to use the marks of others carefully, but they may have a very good legal reason—the preservation of their rights—to challenge any misuse of those marks.

Because a trademark represents the reputation in the marketplace of the products or services of the company that owns it, it may be that company's most valuable asset. It is understandable that trademark owners pay close attention when their marks are used by people they never met in ways they don't necessarily approve. That's why they spend time writing letters to people who misuse them and money to publish ads to explain proper trademark usage. The way to avoid trouble when using other people's trademarks is to handle them like you would handle other people's money— carefully.

❖

CHAPTER 9

Trademarks in Cyberspace

IKE ALL FRONTIERS, cyberspace is largely populated by mavericks and rebels who like the cyber-atmosphere of "if you can imagine it, you can do it." Unfortunately, the very dearth of rules that makes cyberspace so intriguing to everyone who has something to say or sell electronically is also causing problems. Americans often complain about overregulation by local, state, and federal governmental agencies and authorities. But many who are familiar with the problems that have arisen as everybody and his brother scramble for domain names would agree that, in some corners of cyberspace, *more* rules are needed.

One aspect of cyber-commerce has produced disputes for which there is as yet no clear law; this is the ownership of domain names. A domain name is the heart of an e-mail address. In the e-mail address *johnjones@jonesventures.com*, *"jonesventures.com"* is the domain name. Domain names tell Internet users where to find companies and individuals in cyberspace. They function like ZIP codes do for "snail mail"; they direct e-mail and other communications to the right cyberspace neighborhood to find the person or entity named in the first part of the e-mail address. They allow Internet users to visit World Wide Web pages.

The system of categorizing Internet user addresses according to type is familiar to most Net surfers. The five major nonmilitary domains are *.com* for commercial entities, *.gov* for governmental bodies, *.edu* for educational institutions, *.org* for organizations, and *.net* for networks. Because innovative marketers are finding ways to sell everything from coffee to books online, the most crowded part of cyberspace is the commercial district, where all the *.com* addresses are located.

Internet addresses are actually a series of numbers. However, because people who want to locate an Internet merchant are much more likely to remember a verbal address than a series of numbers, domain names are alpha and/or numeric names that a computer can convert to numeric addresses. There is presently no complete directory of domain names. This means that the best domain names look like the names of the companies that own them; this sort of domain name creates an expectation as to who is at the Internet address it names. If you are familiar with a company and its domain name resembles the name of the company, you know what you will find at its address on the Internet. Such Internet addresses are easy to guess and easy to remember. For example, because *ibm.com* is one of the elements of the Internet address for IBM, anyone can guess that that address belongs to that company.

Obstacles on the Superhighway

So far, trademark disputes have been one of the biggest impediments facing Internet marketers. The gist of trademark law is that every marketer is entitled to his or her own reputation in the marketplace. Any interference with this—any act that causes consumers to confuse the products or services of one marketer with those of another—is trademark infringement. Although the legal status of domain names is not yet a settled area of the law, anyone who understands trademark law would agree that domain names are more than just virtual street addresses.

Problems with domain names usually arise when one company

registers a domain name that is identical or similar to the name of another company. It is reasonable that a company whose name has been adopted as the domain name of another enterprise would feel that its rights in its trademark—the embodiment of its commercial reputation—have been infringed. Courts are likely to agree. One variety of trademark infringement is confusion of sponsorship or affiliation. If, on account of similarities between a domain name and the name of an unrelated company, consumers are likely to believe that there is some relationship between the owner of the domain name and the company, the company's trademark rights have been infringed.

Superhighway Robbery

Trademark disputes have, in recent years, resulted when competitors and pranksters have registered domain names that are logically related to the names of established companies. Many such domain-name registrations were apparently made for the purpose of extorting fat buyouts from rich corporations. A journalist registered the domain name *mcdonalds.com* as a part of his research for an article for *Wired* magazine. Needless to say, McDonald's was chagrined to find that the most obvious domain name it could choose had already been registered. Some overeager capitalist at Sprint Communications registered *mci.com*; not surprisingly, MCI Telecommunications objected. The Princeton Review, a leading test-preparation company, registered *kaplan.com*, a domain name based on the name of its competitor, Stanley Kaplan Review, and planned to set up a Web site that compared the two companies' products, presumably showing the alleged inferiority of the Kaplan products. The domain name *mtv.com* was registered and used by a former MTV employee. The domain names *windows95.com* and *nyt.com* were registered by people who were not connected with Microsoft and the *New York Times*. Although several of these "land grabs" resulted in lawsuits, there are no reported court decisions to guide those who will face similar issues because all these disputes were settled out of court. Most of the terms of the settlements in the disputes, including any amounts paid the domain-name hijackers, were not disclosed, but it is telling that all the companies that complained because someone else had registered versions of their names now *own* those domain names.

Similar problems have arisen when companies have registered domain names they had no intention of using. This has been done in the hope that some company that does want to use one of the registered domain names will buy it from the original registrant. This sort of kidnapping has been fairly common.

Eventually there will be a larger body of case law to guide lawyers on these issues because there will certainly be more disputes between trademark owners and cyberspace profiteers and pirates. One reason that more such disputes are likely is that many companies seem unaware of the race for domain names and have been dilatory in registering versions of their corporate names as domain names.

Superhighway Patrol

Formerly, the U.S. government's National Science Foundation assigned all Internet domain names, both military and nonmilitary. As the Net grew, this job became a big one. The National Science Foundation created the InterNIC (the Internet Network Information Center) project to provide Internet management services. The National Science Foundation entered into a contract with a Herndon, Virginia, telecommunications network integration company called Network Solutions, Inc. (NSI) and delegated to NSI the tasks of allocating and managing the registration of nonmilitary domain names.

In 1993, there were only 8,700 registered domain names; by mid-1996, NSI had registered more than 400,000. Currently, NSI handles about 15,000 domain-name registrations each month. Most of these applications for new domain names come from private business—companies are eager to stake their claims to cyberspace territory. For example, Procter and Gamble has registered more than 200 domain names, including *dandruff.com*, *badbreath.com*, and *underarm.com*. Kraft has registered 150 domain names.

In mid-1995, NSI announced a new policy on the registration of domain names. This new policy attempted to end some of the abuses and disputes that had become familiar to would-be Internet marketers. Names were still assigned on a first-come, first-served basis, but, for the first time, an applicant had to represent to NSI that he or she had the legal right to use the name sought to be registered, had a bona fide intention to use the name, and had no unlawful purpose in seeking to register the name. If the owner of a registered trademark objected to another entity's registration of a domain name, the trademark owner could challenge the registration. NSI would then put a "hold" on the domain name, suspending its use until the dispute was resolved. The registration for the domain name was rescinded if the domain-name registrant could not show ownership of a trademark registration for the mark. If both the domain-name registrant and the objecting trademark owner could prove ownership of trademark registrations, the first company to register the trademark as a domain name was awarded the domain name. This situation sometimes occurred in disputes in which registrations in various jurisdictions were involved. The questions arose whether federal registrations should be given priority over state registrations, as is the settled protocol in U.S. trademark law, and what weight should be given to registrations in other countries.

NSI's new policy worked in most cases. However, it did not solve all the problems that can arise between owners of trademarks and would-be registrants of similar domain names, especially in situations where the trademark and domain name are used by companies that are not directly competitive. Inconsistencies between U.S. trademark law and NSI's rules and policies led to several lawsuits involving trademark owners, would-be domain-name registrants, and NSI. NSI, which originally contemplated its role with regard to the Internet as being merely the registrar of domain names, found itself cast, by default, as referee between marketers competing for the same domain names. Since its rules and policies do not have the clout or effect of law, and it is incapable of enforcing its decisions in the way court decisions can be enforced, NSI was anxious to avoid this role and the liability inherent in it.

In an effort to solve some of these problems, in August 1996, NSI announced important revisions, effective in September of that year, to its Domain Name Policy Statement. The revised NSI policy institutes three important changes in the way that domain names are registered:

1. a federal trademark registration obtained after a dispute arises between competitors for a domain name will not provide grounds for obtaining or avoiding an NSI suspension of the domain name in dispute (this means that a domain-name owner will no longer be able to quickly apply for and obtain a foreign registration in an effort to counter a trademark owner's claims that the domain name infringes its rights in the trademark);

2. NSI will not suspend use of a domain name if either the would-be domain-name registrant or the trademark owner files a lawsuit in the dispute over the domain name (if such litigation is commenced, NSI will "deposit control of the domain name into the registry of the court," thereby passing the hot potato to the pertinent court, which will have judicial power to dispose of ownership of the domain name as it sees fit); and

3. NSI will abide by any court order (thereby dispensing with its prior policy of giving equal weight to decisions of the American Arbitration Association) as long as NSI is not itself named as a litigant and, if named, NSI "reserves the right to raise any and all defenses deemed appropriate."

In addition, NSI continues to give preference to owners of trademarks registered federally in the United States, but will now suspend use of a disputed domain name only on the basis of the ownership of a Principal Register federal registration, which is like a first-class federal trademark registration as opposed to a second-class, and less powerful, Supplemental Register registration. NSI will continue to give equal weight to foreign federal trademark registrations as that given U.S. federal registrations.

Trademark owners may also use the expanded protection offered by the new federal Trademark Dilution Act to stop domain-name hijacking. This act will eliminate, for the owners of truly famous marks, the obstacle presented by the use of their marks as domain names by the marketers of noncompeting goods and services.

NSI's newest policy is a big improvement, but it won't solve every problem that will arise involving trademarks and the Internet. Nor will the Trademark Dilution Act, which is really useful only to the owners of demonstrably famous trademarks. Until the law of domain names has become a settled part of trademark law, the best course for any marketer is to immediately register any domain name under which you want to conduct business—or *may* want to conduct business—on the Internet. Stay away from any domain name that you know to be similar to the name or trademark of any other company, especially if that company is a competitor. And because the misuse and use without permission of trademarks in the *content* of Web pages seems likely to grow into another thriving area of trademark infringement, be very careful how you use trademarks that you don't own. An example of content-based trademark infringement would be language in a Web page text that falsely implies a connection between a famous product and the product of the Web site marketer.

Signing Up and Signing On

Applications to register new domain names in the United States may be submitted electronically to InterNIC Registration Services. (Other entities are responsible for registering domain names in the more than 120 other world jurisdictions.) You can call InterNIC at 703/ 742-4777 for information concerning registering a domain name or send an e-mail message to *admin@ds.internic.net*. You can also access this information at *rs.internic.net/contact.html*. If the name you choose is already in use, InterNIC will ask you to choose another. Otherwise, if InterNIC does not deem your name offensive, obscene, or otherwise objectionable, the system will process your application, send it back to you for verification, and tell you when you can begin to use your new name.

InterNIC's exclusive contract with the National Science Foundation expires in March of 1998. Other organizations and groups are already proposing new methods of handling the issuance and registration of domain names, including initiating the use of more categories of domain names, such as *.firm* for businesses, *.store* for merchants, *.web* for Web-related activities, *.arts* for cultural and entertainment sites, *.rec* for recreation and entertainment sites, *.info* for informational services, and *.nom* for individuals. However, there are many problems to be solved and competing interests to be considered before all the questions involved in creating and managing a working worldwide system for domain names are resolved. Stay tuned.

Appendix

A. Trademark Cease and Desist Letter

Romano and Tortellini, Attorneys
205 Waterman Street • Belmont, CA 52245
775/123-4567

October 6, 1997

Mr. Robert Wilson
Mountain Properties, Inc.
729 East Mountain View Drive
Williamsville, CO 72984

VIA REGISTERED MAIL

Dear Mr. Wilson,

This firm represents Brown Management Corporation of Blair, Colorado. Brown Management owns three resort hotels in Colorado: the Brown House Hotel in Denver, the Greenview Hotel in Blair, and the Brownstone Inn in Hopewell, which is, as you know, just over the county line from Williamsville. It is with regard to the Brownstone Inn that I am writing.

Brown Management Corporation has owned and operated the Brownstone Inn since 1954. Over the years, Brown Management has expended a great deal of money to advertise the Brownstone Inn and to ensure that the services and facilities there are the finest available. Consequently, the Brownstone Inn has an excellent reputation, both within Colorado and nationally, as a luxury hotel. Brown Management is the owner of two service marks, both of which have been registered in the United States Patent and Trademark Office. These service marks are the famous name BROWNSTONE INN, which is the subject of federal registration 1,985,065, and the well-known Brownstone Inn script logo, which is the subject of federal registration 1,985,094. Copies of these two registrations are attached to this letter.

It has come to the attention of our client that your corporation has begun construction on a Williamsville time-share condominium development that you intend to call and, indeed, are already calling in advertisements in national travel magazines and in publicity of other kinds, "the Brown Stone Community." Your use of the name "Brown Stone Community" for your resort condominium development constitutes infringement of our client's registered service marks and unfair competition, since consumers may mistake your condominiums for our client's famous hotel or mistakenly believe that your condominiums and our client's hotel have the same owners or that your development is sponsored by or affiliated with Brown Management Corporation or the Brownstone Inn. Furthermore, your use of the "Brown Stone Community" for your development dilutes the strength of our client's famous marks and damages the business reputation and diminishes the good will of the Brownstone Inn, all of which were developed and acquired by our client at great expense and effort.

You should be aware that the United States trademark statute (15 U.S.C. 1051 *et seq.*) provides in part that:

> When a violation of any right of the registrant of a mark registered in the Patent and Trademark Office shall have been established in any civil action arising under this chapter, the plaintiff shall be entitled . . . to recover (1) defendant's profits, (2) any damages sustained by the plaintiff, and (3) the costs of the action.

The law also allows the court to award treble damages and reasonable attorney's fees to the prevailing party. In addition, the court may order that all labels, signs, packaging, and advertisements in the possession of the defendant that bear the registered mark or a colorable imitation thereof be delivered up and destroyed.

Therefore, on behalf of our client, we hereby demand that you immediately cease any uses of the name "Brown Stone Community" or any other imitation or version of our client's registered marks in connection with any present or projected condominium development. Our client will require destruction of any printed advertising or promotion materials bearing the infringing name, including brochures and signage. In addition, your corporation must agree to cease giving out any news stories or causing any advertisements to be published or promulgating any materials connected with the offering of your condominiums that contain any reference to those condominiums as the "Brown Stone Community" development.

Due to the serious nature of your infringing conduct, we require your response to our demands not later than ten days after your receipt of this letter. If you agree to our terms, we will forward an appropriate settlement agreement for execution by an officer of your corporation. If we do not hear from you within ten days or if you refuse to comply with our demands, we are authorized by our client Brownstone Management Corporation to commence an action in federal court on its behalf seeking an injunction, damages, your profits, our costs and attorney's fees, and all other relief allowed by law, without further notice to you.

Although we are hopeful that we can obtain satisfaction for our client without litigation, this letter is written without prejudice to our client's rights and remedies, all of which are expressly reserved.

Sincerely,
Romano and Tortellini, Attorneys

Hubert Tortellini

Hubert Tortellini

HR/tb
attachments: federal trademark registrations 1,985,065 and 1,985,094

B. Trademark Search Opinion Letter

Romano and Tortellini, Attorneys
205 Waterman Street • Belmont, CA 52245
775/123-4567

May 22, 1997

Wil St. Charles, Marketing Director
Fast Foods, Inc.
7 Wilson Pike Circle, Suite 728
St. Paul, MN 71951

Dear Mr. St. Charles,

I am writing to give you my evaluation of the results of the trademark search you recently had me commission for your proposed mark YESTERYEARS for restaurant services. Based on the data produced by that search, I believe that you must find another name for your new hamburger restaurant.

To understand fully the reasons behind my evaluation, you must know something about the principles of trademark infringement. In the United States, trademark rights are acquired by use of the mark. The first person or company to use a trademark gains by that use superior rights in that mark as used for the particular goods or services it names. A new name for a similar product or service will infringe an established mark if the new mark is so similar to the established mark in the way it looks, the way it sounds when spoken, and in its meaning as to be likely to confuse consumers. This standard for trademark infringement is called "confusing similarity." In your case, your proposed use of YESTERYEARS for hamburger restaurant services would infringe any very similar, older trademark that names *any type* of restaurant, since consumers could easily believe that the restaurants were owned or franchised by the same organization.

Because federal trademark registration enhances the rights that accrue to trademark owners by use of their marks, trademarks that are registered federally are the most important class of marks to avoid infringing. However, the rights of state trademark registrants and those of owners of established but unregistered marks are just as valid and must also be taken into account when assessing the availability for use of a proposed mark, although the owners of those marks may not have used their marks widely enough to gain extensive rights in them.

There are several federal registrations listed in the search report for YESTERYEARS for marks that include a form of YESTERYEAR as an element. However, none of these prior registrations would present a problem to your proposed use of YESTERYEARS because, as you will note when you examine the search report, the marks all name products (costume jewelry, picture frames, etc.) that are very different from restaurant services.

However, there is a federal registration for YESTERDAY'S for restaurant services, as well as one for YESTERDOG, also for restaurant services. Both of these registrations are currently valid and in force, according to the information in the search report. In my opinion, your proposed use of YESTERYEARS for restaurant services would infringe the rights of the YESTERDAY'S trademark owners because your proposed mark could be confused with that registered mark. In addition, there is a notation in the YESTERDAY'S entry in the search report that the owners of YESTERDAY'S filed an opposition against the federal registration of YESTERDOG for restaurant services. This opposition proceeding was dropped, but the fact that it was filed indicates the vigilance with which the owners of YESTERDAY'S oppose what they consider infringements.

The state registrations section of the search report lists one YESTERYEARS registration, for restaurant services, in Massachusetts. There are also two Tennessee registrations for YESTERDAY'S, as well as Kansas and California registrations for YESTERDAY'S; all are for restaurant services. All the marks that are the subjects of these state registrations could be infringed by your proposed use of YESTERYEARS. In the trade names section of the report, which reflects phone directory listings and other occurrences of business names similar to your proposed mark, there are listings for fourteen restaurants, the names for which start with the word YESTER-YEARS. There are even more listings (several pages) for restaurants that use the word YESTERDAYS in their names. Any of the restaurants named YESTERYEARS or using YESTERYEARS as a part of their name could pose a threat to your use of the name.

I am sorry the news is bad. Apparently, others have discovered before you that YESTERYEARS is a good name. Finding out the bad news now is preferable to finding it out by means of a cease and desist letter.

When you decide what new name you would like to use in place of YESTERYEARS, call me. We can order expedited service on the new search report in order to have it delivered very quickly.

I enclose a copy of the YESTERYEARS search report.

Please call me if you have questions.

Sincerely,
Romano and Tortellini, Attorneys

Sigrid Romano

Sigrid Romano

SR/tb
enclosure

Trademark Search Report (Summary)

Search:	771951	Mark Searched:	YESTERYEARS
Goods/Services:	restaurant services	Type of Search:	full search
Date of Search:	May 15, 1997		

FEDERAL REGISTRATIONS

1.	R12984	YESTER-YEAR PRODUCTS
2.	R53847	YESTERYEAR JEWELRY DESIGNS
3.	R54092	YESTERYEAR LOG HOMES
4.	R55772	MODELS OF YESTERYEAR

5.	R09803	THE COLLECTOR'S CHOICE YESTERYEAR, TODAY, AND THEREAFTER
6.	R33720	TOMORROW'S IDEAS YESTERYEAR'S CRAFTSMANSHIP
7.	R96022	YESTERYEAR, LTD.
8.	R00493	VIDEO YESTERYEAR
9.	R34986	RADIO YESTERYEAR
10.	R32098	YESTERYEAR
11.	R49763	ARTISANS & CRAFTSMEN PRESENTS YESTERYEAR
12.	R98323	RADIOS OF YESTERYEAR
13.	R79595	RIDE BACK INTO YESTERYEAR
14.	R93897	A GRAND HOTEL, YESTERDAY, TODAY, AND TOMORROW
15.	R69672	HOPPER'S DRIVE-INN "AT HOPPER'S YESTERDAY IS BETTER THAN EVER!"
16.	R10919	YESTERDAY'S
17.	R36091	YESTERDOG
18.	R99884	YESTER-LAID
19.	R34430	YESTERDAY'S EGGS DELIVERED TODAY
20.	R43513	YESTA
21.	R07999	YESTERYEAR FRAMES
22.	R34005	GOOD YEAR
23.	R35639	TENDER YEARS
24.	R59692	SALAD OF THE YEAR
25.	R23892	GOOD FOOD FOR MORE THAN 40 YEARS

C. Trademark Search Opinion Letter (Second Search)

Romano and Tortellini, Attorneys
205 Waterman Street • Belmont, CA 52245
775/123-4567

June 18, 1997

Wil St. Charles, Marketing Director
Fast Foods, Inc.
7 Wilson Pike Circle, Suite 728
St. Paul, MN 71951

Dear Mr. St. Charles,

I am writing to give you my evaluation of the results of the trademark search I commissioned for you for your second proposed mark for restaurant services, THE SOUTHERN BURGER COMPANY. Based on the data produced by that search, I believe that you will encounter no opposition to your proposed use of THE SOUTHERN BURGER COMPANY and may safely adopt the mark.

Trademark infringement is caused by "confusing similarity" between two marks and is judged by the "sight, sound, and meaning" test. That is, do the two marks look so alike and sound so alike and have such similar meanings that they are likely to be confused by consumers if they name similar products or services? Applying this standard, I believe that none of the marks reported in the latest search report will be infringed by your use of THE SOUTHERN BURGER COMPANY for hamburger restaurant services.

Although the words "southern," "south," and "burger" are formative verbal elements in many of the marks reported, the degree of similarity in the entire name in each case is such that there is no confusing similarity. For this reason, there are no federally registered marks that concern me.

The state registration for BURGER COMPANY on page 2 of the state listings section of the report is, I believe, of little concern. This is probably only a local restaurant; the owners would have a very hard time claiming infringement since their BURGER COMPANY is a generic or descriptive mark that is not accorded a wide degree of protection. The same goes for SOUTHERN BIG BURGER on page 1 of the trade names section of the report.

I must remind you that although this is the most reliable information available to us, it may not be absolutely complete. It is always possible that there is some valid but unregistered trademark that would be infringed by your proposed mark that did not show up in this search report because it is unregistered. That does not happen often, but it is a possibility.

I have enclosed a copy of the search report for your examination. Please call me if you have questions.

Sincerely,
Romano and Tortellini, Attorneys

Sigrid Romano

SR/tb
enclosure

Trademark Search Report (Summary)

Search: 771997   Mark Searched: THE SOUTHERN BURGER COMPANY

Goods/Services: restaurant services   Type of Search: full search

Date of Search: June 3, 1997

FEDERAL REGISTRATIONS

1. R12916 SOUTH STREET SAUSAGE
2. R93147 SOUTH PHILLY STEAKS & FRIES
3. R00092 SOUTHSIDE BURGERS
4. R51772 THE BIGGER BURGER COMPANY
5. R09100 WESTERN CHEESEBURGER
6. R31720 LOUISIANA GROCERY & FEED COMPANY
7. R56023 THE MISSISSIPPI RIVER COMPANY
8. R09453 THE GREAT LAKES STEAK COMPANY
9. R34917 CALIFORNIA CASTLE BURGER
10. R35091 SOUTH-OF-THE-BORDER BURGERS
11. R35765 SOUTHERN SUN
12. R91323 SOUTHERN HOSPITALITY CORPORATION
13. R49554 SOUTHERN SPORTSMAN
14. R23197 SOUTHWEST CHILI
15. R45671 SOUTH SHORE HARBOR
16. R00912 SOUTHERN SKILLET
17. R36091 THE SOUTHERN COOKER HOME STYLE RESTAURANT
18. R09119 SOUTHERN BELLE
19. R54430 SOUTHERN GEM
20. R43511 SOUTHERN CHEF
21. R17995 THE TASTE THE SOUTH LOVES
22. R34009 PUT SOME SOUTH IN YOUR MOUTH
23. R55632 BLUE BOAR SERVING RIVER CITIES OF THE SOUTH
24. R55621 COLEMAN'S BAR-B-Q SOUTH'S FINEST
25. R33124 DIXIE KITCHEN SOUTHERN FRIED CHICKEN
26. R30913 FANDANGO'S SOUTHWESTERN CHAR GRILL
27. R84356 THE FLAVOR OF THE DEEP SOUTH
28. R19995 JOSE'S SOUTHWEST AMERICAN CANTINA
29. R57833 BURGER KING
30. R76340 MR. BURGER
31. R49877 THE ALL AMERICAN BURGER
32. R56226 BAGELBURGER
33. R99001 BABY BURGER
34. R91556 BUN N' BURGER
35. R12390 CIRCUS BURGERS
36. R56700 DIXIE BURGER
37. R37677 IN-N-OUT BURGERS
38. R39288 THE ALL AMERICAN BURGER

39.	R32009	NORTH AMERICAN LOBSTER COMPANY
40.	R73552	CONSOLIDATED FOODS COMPANY
41.	R93117	BABY DOE MINING COMPANY
42.	R33182	BOSTON SEAFOOD COMPANY
44.	R66743	BREAD & COMPANY
45.	R22910	CALHOUN STREET OYSTER COMPANY
46.	R53267	CHICAGO SANDWICH COMPANY
47.	R10927	GREAT AMERICAN PIZZA COMPANY
48.	R39917	SOUTHERN
49.	R21803	SOUTHERN FOODS
50.	R39920	BURGER BURGER
51.	R33209	BEST BURGERS

D. Directory of State Trademark Agencies

Alabama
Secretary of State
Lands and Trademark Division
State Office Building, Room 528
Montgomery, AL 36130
205/242-7200

Alaska
Department of Commerce and
    Economic Development
Corporations Section
P.O. Box D
Juneau, AK 99811
907/465-2530

Arizona
Office of Secretary of State
1700 West Washington Street
Phoenix, AZ 85007
602/542-61877

Arkansas
Secretary of State
State Capital Building
Little Rock, AR 72201-1094
501/682-3622

California
Secretary of State
Trademark Unit
State of California
1230 J Street
Sacramento, CA 95814
916/445-9872

Colorado
Secretary of State
Corporations Office
1560 Broadway, Suite 200
Denver, CO 80202
303/894-2251

Connecticut
Secretary of State
Division of Corporations, UCC and
    Trademarks
Attention: Trademarks
30 Trinity Street
Hartford, CT 06106
203/566-1721

Delaware
Department of State
Division of Corporations
Attention: Trademark Filings
Townsend Building
P.O. Box 898
Dover, DE 19903
302/736-3073

Florida
Corporation Records Bureau
Division of Corporations
Department of State
P.O. Box 6327
Tallahassee, FL 32301
904/487-6000

Georgia
Secretary of State
306 West Floyd Towers
2 Martin Luther King Drive
Atlanta, GA 30334
404/656-2861

Hawaii
Department of Commerce and
    Consumer Affairs
Business Registration Division
1010 Richards Street
Honolulu, HI 96813
808/548-6111

Idaho
Secretary of State
Statehouse, Room 203
Boise, ID 83720
208/334-2300

Illinois
Secretary of State
The Index Department
Trademark Division
111 East Monroe

Springfield, IL 62756
217/782-7017

Indiana
Secretary of State
Trademark Division
State House, Room 155
Indianapolis, IN 46204
317/232-6540

Iowa
Secretary of State
Corporate Division
Hoover Building
Des Moines, IA 50319
515/281-5204

Kansas
Secretary of State
Statehouse Building, Room 235N
Topeka, KS 66612
913/296-2236

Kentucky
Secretary of State
State Capitol, Room 150
Frankfort, KY 40601-3493
502/564-2848

Louisiana
Secretary of State
Corporation Division
P.O. Box 94125
Baton Rouge, LA 70804-9125
504/925-4698

Maine
Department of State
Division of Public Administration
State House Station 101

Augusta, ME 04333
207/289-3501

Maryland
Secretary of State
State House
Annapolis, MD 21404
301/974-5521

Massachusetts
Secretary of State
Trademark Division
1 Ashburton Place
Room 1711
Boston, MA 02108
617/727-8329

Michigan
Department of Commerce
Corporations and Securities Bureau
Corporation Division
P.O. Box 30054
Lansing, MI 48909
517/334-6302

Minnesota
Secretary of State
Corporations Division
180 State Office Building
St. Paul, MN 55155
612/296-3266

Mississippi
Secretary of State
P.O. Box 1350
Jackson, MS 39215
601/359-1350

Missouri
Secretary of State

Trademark Division
P.O. Box 778
Jefferson City, MO 65101
314/751-4756

Montana
Secretary of State
Montana State Capitol
Helena, MT 59620
406/444-3665

Nebraska
Secretary of State
State Capitol Building
Lincoln, NE 68509
402/471-4079

Nevada
Secretary of State
Capitol Complex
Carson City, NV 89710
702/687-5203

New Hampshire
Corporations Division
Secretary of State
State House Annex
Concord, NH 03301
603/271-4244

New Jersey
Secretary of State
State House
CN-300
West State Street
Trenton, NJ 08625
609/984-1900

New Mexico
Secretary of State
Capitol Building, Room 400
Santa Fe, NM 87503

505/827-3600

New York
Secretary of State
Department of State
Miscellaneous Records
162 Washington Avenue
Albany, NY 12231
518/474-4770

North Carolina
Secretary of State
Trademark Division
300 North Salisbury Street
Raleigh, NC 27611
919/733-4161

North Dakota
Secretary of State
State Capitol
Bismarck, ND 58505
701/224-2900

Ohio
Secretary of State
Corporations Department
30 East Broad Street, 14th Floor
Columbus, OH 43215-0418
614/466-3910

Oklahoma
Secretary of State
State of Oklahoma
101 State Capitol Building
Oklahoma City, OK 73105
405/521-3911

Oregon
Secretary of State
Director, Corporation Division

158 Twelfth Street, NE
Salem, OR 97310-0210
503/378-3478

Pennsylvania
Secretary of State
Corporation Bureau
309 North Office Building
Harrisburg, PA 17120
717/787-2004

Puerto Rico
Secretary of State
P.O. Box 3271
San Juan, PR 00904
809/722-2121

Rhode Island
Secretary of State
Trademarks Division
100 North Main Street
Providence, RI 02903
401/277-2521

South Carolina
Secretary of State
P.O. Box 11350
Columbia, SC 29211
803/758-2744

South Dakota
Secretary of State
State Capitol Building
500 East Capitol
Pierre, SD 57501
605/773-3537

Tennessee
Secretary of State
James K. Polk Building, Suite 500
Nashville, TN 37219
615/741-0531

Texas
Secretary of State
Corporations Section
Trademark Office
Box 13697, Capitol Station
Austin, TX 78711-3697
512/463-5576

Utah
Division of Corporations and
    Commercial Code
Heber M. Wells Building
160 East South Street
Salt Lake City, UT 84111
801/532-6935

Vermont
Secretary of State
Corporations Division
Redstone Building
26 Terrace Street
Mail: State Office Building
Montpelier, VT 05602-2199
802/828-2386

Virginia
State Corporations Commission
Division of Securities and Retail
    Franchises
1220 Bank Street
Richmond, VA 23209
804/786-7751

Washington
Secretary of State
Corporations Division
Republic Building, Second Floor
505 East Union Street
Olympia, WA 98504
206/753-7120

West Virginia
Secretary of State
Corporations Division
State Capitol
Charleston, WV 25305
304/342-8000

Wisconsin
Secretary of State
Trademark Records
P.O. Box 7848
Madison, WI 53707
608/266-5653

Wyoming
Secretary of State
Corporations Divison
Capitol Building
Cheyenne, WY 82002
307/777-7378

BASIC FACTS ABOUT
TRADEMARKS

U. S. Department of Commerce • Patent and Trademark Office • Washington, DC 20231

*T*his booklet contains the information and forms you need to register a trademark for a product or service. If you need additional information about the process, call 1-800-PTO-9199 or our Trademark Assistance Center at 703-308-9000.

What is a trademark?

It is a word, phrase, symbol or design, or combination of words, phrases, symbols or designs, which identifies and distinguishes the source of the goods or services of one party from those of others. A service mark is the same as a trademark, except that it identifies and distinguishes the source of a service rather than a product. In this booklet, the terms "trademark" and "mark" are used to refer to both trademarks and service marks, whether they are word marks or other types of marks. Normally, a mark for goods appears on the product or on its packaging, while a service mark appears in advertising for the services.

A trademark is different from a copyright or a patent. A copyright protects an original artistic or literary work; a patent protects an invention. For copyright information, call the Library of Congress at (202) 707-3000.

How do I establish trademark rights?

Trademark rights arise from either (1) actual use of the mark, or (2) the filing of a proper application to register a mark in the Patent and Trademark Office (PTO) stating that the applicant has a bona fide intention to use the mark in commerce regulated by the U.S. Congress. (See below, under "Types of Applications," for a discussion of what is meant by

the terms "commerce" and "use in commerce.") Federal registration is not required to establish rights in a mark, nor is it required to begin use of a mark. However, federal registration can secure benefits beyond the rights acquired by merely using a mark. For example, the owner of a federal registration is presumed to be the owner of the mark for the goods and services specified in the registration, and to be entitled to use the mark nationwide.

There are two related but distinct types of rights in a mark: the right to register and the right to use. Generally, the first party who either uses a mark in commerce or files an application in the PTO has the ultimate right to register that mark. The PTO's authority is limited to determining the right to register. The right to use a mark can be more complicated to determine. This is particularly true when two parties have begun use of the same or similar marks without knowledge of one another and neither has a federal registration. Only a court can render a decision about the right to use, such as issuing an injunction or awarding damages for infringement. It should be noted that a federal registration can provide significant advantages to a party involved in a court proceeding. The PTO cannot provide advice concerning rights in a mark. Only a private attorney can provide such advice.

1

How do I maintain my trademark registration?

Unlike copyrights or patents, trademark rights can last indefinitely if the owner continues to use the mark to identify its goods or services. The term of a federal trademark registration is 10 years, with 10-year renewal terms. A renewal application for a trademark registration **cannot be filed until at least 6 months prior to the expiration of the trademark registration.**

However, between the fifth and sixth year after the date of initial registration, **the registrant must file an affidavit or declaration** setting forth the following information in order to keep the registration alive.

(1) An affidavit or declaration, which must include a specific list of the goods or services recited in the registration, averring that the registrant is still using the mark on or in connection with the goods or services listed;

(2) A specimen showing how the mark is currently in use with the goods or services identified, e.g., a tag, label or package for goods, or an advertisement for a service; and

(3) the required filing fee.

If no affidavit or declaration is filed, the registration is canceled. Please note that you will not receive any advance notice from the Office that the Affidavit or Declaration of Continued Use must be filed by a certain date. Since fees are subject to change over time, registrants are strongly encouraged to call the Post Registration Section of the Office (phone number on page 4) to determine the proper fee or to ask specific questions about the procedures to follow when it becomes time to file either the Affidavit or Declaration of Continued Use or Renewal Application.

What type of application do I need?

Applicants may apply for federal registration in three principal ways:

(1) An applicant who has already started using a mark in commerce may file based on that use (a "use" application).

(2) An applicant who has not yet used the mark may apply based on a bona fide intention to use the mark in commerce (an "intent-to-use" application). For the purpose of obtaining federal registration, "commerce" means all commerce which may lawfully be regulated by the U.S. Congress - for example, interstate commerce or commerce between the U.S. and another country. The use in commerce must be a bona fide use in the ordinary course of trade, and not made merely to reserve a right in a mark. Use of a mark in promotion or advertisement before the product or service is actually provided under the mark on a normal commercial scale does not qualify as use in commerce. Use of a mark in purely local commerce within a state does not qualify as "use in commerce." If an applicant files based on a bona fide intention to use in commerce, the applicant will have to use the mark in commerce and submit an amendment to allege use or statement of use to the PTO before the PTO will register the mark.

(3) Additionally, under certain international agreements, an applicant from outside the United States may file in the United States based on an application or registration in another country. For information regarding applications based on international agreements please call the information number provided on page 4.

A United States registration provides protection only in the United States and its territories. If the owner of a mark wishes to protect a mark in other countries, the owner must seek protection in each country separately under the relevant laws. The PTO cannot provide information or advice concerning protection in other countries. Interested parties may inquire directly in the relevant country or its U.S. offices or through an attorney.

Who may file an application?

The application must be filed in the name of the owner of the mark; usually an individual, corporation or partnership. The owner of a mark controls the nature and quality of the goods or services identified by the mark. See below in the line-by-line instructions for information about who must sign the application and other papers.

The owner may submit and prosecute its own application for registration, or may be represented by an attorney. The PTO cannot help select an attorney.

What about foreign applicants?

Applicants not living in the United States must designate in writing the name and address of a domestic representative — a person residing in the United States "upon whom notices of process may be served for proceedings affecting the mark." The applicant may do so by submitting a statement that the named person at the address indicated is appointed as the applicant's domestic representative under §1(e) of the Trademark Act. The applicant must sign this statement. This person will receive all communications from the PTO unless the applicant is represented by an attorney in the United States.

Do I need to search for conflicting marks?

An applicant is not required to conduct a search for conflicting marks prior to applying with the PTO. However, some people find it useful. In evaluating an application, an examining attorney conducts a search and notifies the applicant if a conflicting mark is found. **The application fee, which covers processing and search costs, will not be refunded even if a conflict is found and the mark cannot be registered.**

To determine whether there is a conflict between two marks, the PTO determines whether there would be likelihood of confusion, that is, whether relevant consumers would be likely to associate the goods or services of one party with those of the other party as a result of the use of the marks at issue by both parties. The principal factors to be considered in reaching this decision are the similarity of the marks and the commercial relationship between the goods and services identified by the marks. To find a conflict, the marks need not be identical, and the goods and services do not have to be the same.

The PTO does not conduct searches for the public to determine if a conflicting mark is registered, or is the subject of a pending application, except as noted above when acting on an application. However, there are a variety of ways to get this same type of information. First, the applicant may perform a search in the PTO public search library. The search library is located on the second floor of the South Tower Building, 2900 Crystal Drive, Arlington, Virginia 22202. Second, the applicant may visit a patent and trademark depository library (see pages 14 and 15). These libraries have CD-ROM's containing the trademark database of registered and pending marks. Finally, either a private trademark search company, or an attorney who deals with trademark law, can provide trademark registration information. The PTO cannot provide advice about possible conflicts between marks.

What laws and rules govern federal registration?

The federal registration of trademarks is governed by the Trademark Act of 1946, as amended, 15 U.S.C. §1051 et seq.; the Trademark Rules, 37 C.F.R. Part 2; and the Trademark Manual of Examining Procedure (2d ed. 1993).

Are there any other types of applications?

In addition to trademarks and service marks, the Trademark Act provides for federal registration of other types of marks, such as certification marks, collective trademarks and service marks, and collective membership marks. These types of marks are relatively rare. For forms and information regarding the registration of these marks, call one of the information contacts for assistance.

Where do I send the application and correspondence?

The application and all other correspondence should be addressed to "The Assistant Commissioner for Trademarks, 2900 Crystal Drive, Arlington, Virginia 22202-3513." The initial application should be directed to "Box NEW APP / FEE." An AMENDMENT TO ALLEGE USE should be directed to "Attention AAU." A STATEMENT OF USE or REQUEST FOR AN EXTENSION OF TIME TO FILE A STATEMENT OF USE should be directed to "Box ITU / FEE." (See pages 12 and 13 for an explanation of these terms.)

3

The applicant should indicate its telephone number on the application form. Once a serial number is assigned to the application, the applicant should refer to the serial number in all written and telephone communications concerning the application.

It is advisable to submit a stamped, self-addressed postcard with the application specifically listing each item in the mailing, e.g., the written application, the drawing, the fee, and the specimens (if appropriate). The PTO will stamp the filing date and serial number of the application on the postcard to acknowledge receipt. This will help the applicant if any item is later lost or if the applicant wishes to inquire about the application. The PTO will send a separate official notification of the filing date and serial number for every application about one or two months after receipt. It is also recommended that applicants retain a copy of their application, specimens, drawing and any other correspondence mailed to the PTO, along with any proof of mailing, such as Certificates of Mailing or PTO stamped copies showing actual delivery of the materials or correspondence to the Office.

What's the difference between "TM," "SM" and "®" symbols?

Anyone who claims rights in a mark may use the TM (trademark) or SM (service mark) designation with the mark to alert the public to the claim. It is not necessary to have a registration, or even a pending application, to use these designations. The claim may or may not be valid. The registration symbol, ®, may only be used when the mark is registered in the PTO. It is improper to use this symbol at any point before the registration issues. Please omit all symbols from the mark in the drawing you submit with your application; the symbols are not considered part of the mark.

How do I register?

The following sections explain how the registration process works and what requirements are needed to complete a registration application. If you need additional information, call PTO general information at 1-800-PTO-9199 or the Trademark Assistance Center at 703-308-9000.

Important contacts for trademark customers

General Trademark or Patent Information	1-800-PTO-9199
	(703) 308-HELP
Automated (Recorded) General Trademark or Patent Information	1-800-PTO-9199
Automated Line for Status Information on Trademark Applications (Additional status information is available at (703) 308-9400)	(703) 305-8747
Assignment & Certification Branch (Assignments, Changes of Name, and Certified Copies of Applications and Registrations)	(703) 308-9723 Assignments
	(703) 308-9726 Certification
Trademark Assistance Center	(703) 308-9000
Post Registration - Information Regarding Renewals [Sec. 9], Affidavits of Use [Sec. 8], Incontestability [Sec. 15], or Correcting a Mistake on a Registration	(703) 308-9500
Information Regarding Applications Based on International Agreements or for Certification, Collective, or Collective Membership Marks	(703) 308-9000 or
	(703) 308-8900
Trademark Trial and Appeal Board	(703) 308-9300
Assistant Commissioner for Trademarks	(703) 308-8900
PTO WEB SITE	**http://www.uspto.gov**

The Process

Filing Date - Filing Receipt

The PTO is responsible for the federal registration of trademarks. When an application is received, the PTO reviews it to determine if it meets the minimum requirements for receiving a filing date. If the application meets the filing requirements, the PTO assigns it a serial number and sends the applicant a receipt about two months after filing. If the minimum requirements are not met, the entire mailing, including the filing fee, is returned to the applicant.

Examination

About four or five months after filing an application, an examining attorney at the PTO reviews the application and determines whether the mark may be registered. If the examining attorney determines that the mark cannot be registered, the examining attorney will issue a letter listing any grounds for refusal and any corrections required in the application. The examining attorney may also contact the applicant by telephone if only minor corrections are required. The applicant must respond to any objections within six months of the mailing date of the letter, or the application will be abandoned. If the applicant's response does not overcome all objections, the examining attorney will issue a final refusal. The applicant may then appeal to the Trademark Trial and Appeal Board, an administrative tribunal within the PTO.

A common ground for refusal is likelihood of confusion between the applicant's mark and a registered mark. This ground is discussed on page 3. Marks which are merely descriptive in relation to the applicant's goods or services, or a feature of the goods or services, may also be refused. Marks consisting of geographic terms or surnames may also be refused. Marks may be refused for other reasons as well.

Publication for Opposition

If there are no objections, or if the applicant overcomes all objections, the examining attorney will approve the mark for publication in the Official Gazette, a weekly publication of the PTO. The PTO will send a NOTICE OF PUBLICATION to the applicant indicating the date of publication. In the case of two or more applications for similar marks, the PTO will publish the application with the earliest effective filing date first. Any party who believes it may be damaged by the registration of the mark has 30 days from the date of publication to file an opposition to registration. An opposition is similar to a formal proceeding in the federal courts, but is held before the Trademark Trial and Appeal Board. If no opposition is filed, the application enters the next stage of the registration process.

Issuance of Certificate of Registration or Notice of Allowance

If the application was based upon the actual use of the mark in commerce prior to approval for publication, the PTO will register the mark and issue a registration certificate about 12 weeks after the date the mark was published, if no opposition was filed.

If, instead, the mark was published based upon the applicant's statement of having a bona fide intention to use the mark in commerce, the PTO will issue a NOTICE OF ALLOWANCE about 12 weeks after the date the mark was published, again provided no opposition was filed. The applicant then has six months from the date of the NOTICE OF ALLOWANCE to either (1) use the mark in commerce and submit a STATEMENT OF USE, or (2) request a six-month EXTENSION OF TIME TO FILE A STATEMENT OF USE (see forms and instructions in this booklet). The applicant may request additional extensions of time only as noted in the instructions on the back of the extension form. If the STATEMENT OF USE is filed and approved, the PTO will then issue the registration certificate.

Length of Time for Application Processing

It is difficult to provide precise estimates as to how long it takes from the filing of an application to the receipt of a certificate of registration in any particular case, because numerous factors can arise during the examination process which can lengthen the process. For example, if an application is refused because of a prior pending conflicting application, the later-filed application could be suspended for several months or possibly one or two years until the prior-pending conflicting application is either registered or abandoned. Other factors, such as whether the application has been filed based on "intent-to-use," or based on a foreign application, or whether a Notice of

Opposition is filed by a third party, can cause delays. However, if there are no (or relatively minor) substantive or procedural problems, and the application is based on "use in commerce," and no Notice of Opposition is filed by a third party, it may be possible to obtain a registration within 10-12 months of the application filing date. Intent-to-use (ITU) applications which have little or no major problems, and which are not opposed by third parties, could receive a NOTICE OF ALLOWANCE within 10-12 months of the application filing date. However, the ITU application would not be registered until the applicant files an acceptable Statement of Use along with specimens showing the mark in use in commerce.

Filing Requirements

BEFORE COMPLETING AN APPLICATION, READ THE INSTRUCTIONS CAREFULLY AND STUDY THE EXAMPLES PROVIDED. ERRORS OR OMISSIONS MAY RESULT IN THE DENIAL OF A FILING DATE AND THE RETURN OF APPLICATION PAPERS, OR THE DENIAL OF REGISTRATION AND FORFEITURE OF THE FILING FEE.

To receive a filing date, the applicant must provide all of the following:

1. A written application (for example, see PTO FORM 1478);

2. A drawing of the mark on a separate piece of paper;

3. The required filing fee (see pages 11 and 12 for fee information); and

4. If the application is filed based upon prior use of the mark in commerce, three specimens for each class of goods or services. The specimens must show actual use of the mark with the goods or services. The specimens may be identical or they may be examples of three different uses showing the same mark.

1. WRITTEN APPLICATION

The application must be in English. A separate application must be filed for each mark the applicant

wishes to register. Likewise, if the applicant wishes to register more than one version of the same mark, a separate application must be filed for each version. PTO Form 1478 included in the back of this booklet may be used for either a trademark or service mark application. It may be photocopied for your convenience. See the examples of completed applications on pages 18 and 19 with references to the following line-by-line instructions.

LINE-BY-LINE INSTRUCTIONS FOR FILLING OUT PTO FORM 1478, ENTITLED "TRADEMARK/SERVICE MARK APPLICATION, PRINCIPAL REGISTER, WITH DECLARATION"

Space 1 — The Mark

Indicate the mark (for example, "THEORYTEC" or "PINSTRIPES AND DESIGN"). This should agree with the mark shown on the drawing page. If there is a discrepancy between the mark described in the written application and the mark displayed in the drawing, the drawing controls.

Space 2 — Classification

It is not necessary to fill in this box. The PTO will determine the proper International Classification based upon the identification of the goods and services in the application. However, if the applicant knows the International Class number(s) for the goods and services, the applicant may place the number(s) in this box. The International Classes are listed inside of the back cover of this booklet. If the PTO determines that the goods and services listed are in more than one class, the PTO will notify the applicant during examination of the application, and the applicant will have the opportunity to pay the fees for any additional classes or to limit the goods and services to one or more classes.

Space 3 — The Owner of the Mark

The name of the owner of the mark must be entered in this box. The application must be filed in the name of the owner of the mark or the application will be void, and the applicant will forfeit the filing fee.

The owner of the mark is the party who controls the nature and quality of the goods sold, or services rendered, under the mark. The owner may be an individual, a partnership, a corporation, or an association or similar firm. If the applicant is a corporation, the applicant's name is the name under which it is incorporated. If the applicant is a partnership, the applicant's name is the name under which it is organized.

Space 4 — The Owner's Address

Enter the applicant's business address. If the applicant is an individual, enter either the applicant's business or home address. It is very important for applicants to keep the mailing address current with the PTO. If an applicant's mailing address changes at any time during the application process, **applicant must submit a written notice to the PTO requesting that the correspondence address be changed.** The PTO will not accept a change of address by telephone.

Space 5 — Entity Type and Citizenship/Domicile

The applicant must check the box which indicates the type of entity applying. In addition, in the blank following the box, the applicant must specify the following information:

Space 5(a) — for an **individual,** the applicant's national citizenship (married couples should use either space 5(b) if engaged in an organized partnership, or Space 5(d) as "joint applicants.");

Space 5(b) — for a **partnership,** the names and national citizenship's of the general partners and the state where the partnership is organized (if a U.S. partnership) or country (if a foreign partnership);

Space 5(c) — for a **corporation,** the state of incorporation (if a U.S. corporation), or country (if a foreign corporation); or

Space 5(d) — for another type of entity, specify the nature of the entity, such as "joint applicants," "joint ventures" or "Limited Liability Companies

(LLC)", and the state where it is organized (if in the U.S.) or country where it is organized (if a foreign entity), or national citizenship of each "joint applicant."

Space 6 — Identification of the Goods and/or Services

In this blank the applicant must state the specific goods and services for which registration is sought and with which the applicant has actually used the mark in commerce, or in the case of an "intent-to-use" application, has a bona fide intention to use the mark in commerce. Use clear and concise terms specifying the actual goods and services by their common commercial names. A mark can be registered only for specific goods and services. The goods and services listed will establish the scope of the applicant's rights in the relevant mark.

The goods and services listed must be the applicant's actual "goods in trade" or the actual services the applicant renders for the benefit of others. Use language that would be readily understandable to the general public. For example, if the applicant uses or intends to use the mark to identify "candy," "word processors," "baseballs and baseball bats," "travel magazines," "dry cleaning services" or "restaurant services" the identification should clearly and concisely list each such item. If the applicant uses indefinite terms, such as "accessories," "components," "devices," "equipment," "food," "materials," "parts," "systems," "products," or the like, then those words must be followed by the word "namely" and the goods or services listed by their common commercial name(s). Note that the terms used in the classification listing on the inside of the back cover of this booklet are generally too broad. Do not use these terms by themselves.

The applicant must be very careful when identifying the goods and services. Because the filing of an application establishes certain presumptions of rights as of the filing date, the application may not **be amended later to add any products or services not within the scope of the identification.** For example, the identification of "clothing" could be amended to "shirts and jackets," which narrows the scope, but could not be amended to "retail clothing store services," which would change the scope. Similarly, "physical therapy services" could not be changed to "medical services" because this would broaden the scope of the identification. Also, if the identification includes a trade channel limitation, deleting that limitation would broaden the scope of the identification. Furthermore, if goods or services are deleted at any time during the application process by applicant, the deleted goods or services cannot later be reinserted.

The **identification of goods and services** must not describe **the mode or method** of use of the mark, such as on labels, stationery, menus, signs, containers or in advertising. There is another place on the application, called the "method-of-use clause," for this kind of information. (See information under Space 7a, fourth blank, described on the next page.) For example, in the identification of goods and services, the term "advertising" usually is intended to identify a service rendered by advertising agencies. Moreover, "labels," "menus," "signs" and "containers" are specific goods. **If the applicant identifies these goods or services by mistake, the applicant may not amend the identification to the actual goods or services of the applicant.** Thus, if the identification indicates "menus," it could not be amended to "restaurant services." Similarly, if the goods are identified as "containers or labels for jam," the identification could not be amended to "jam."

NOTE: If nothing appears in this blank, or if the identification does not identify any recognizable goods or services, the application will be denied a filing date and returned to the applicant. For example, if the applicant specifies the mark itself or wording such as "company name," "corporate name," or "company logo," and nothing else, the application will be denied a filing date and returned to the applicant. If the applicant identifies the goods and services too broadly as, for example, "advertising and business," "miscellaneous," "miscellaneous goods and services," or just "products," or "services," the application will also be denied a filing date and returned to the applicant.

Space 7 — Basis for Filing

The applicant must check at least one of the four boxes to specify a basis for filing the application. The applicant should also fill in all blanks which follow the checked box(es). Usually an application is based upon either (1) use of the mark in commerce (the first box), or (2) a bona fide intention to use the mark in commerce (the second box). **You may not check both the first and second box. If both the first and second boxes are checked, the PTO will not accept the application and will return it.** If an applicant wishes to apply to register a mark, for certain goods and services for which it is already using the mark in commerce, and also for other goods and services based on future use, separate applications must be filed to separate the relevant goods and services from each other.

Space 7(a)

If the applicant is using the mark in commerce in relation to all of the goods and services listed in the application, check this first box and fill in the blanks.

In the **first blank** specify the date the trademark was first used to identify the goods and services in a type of commerce which may be regulated by Congress.

In the **second blank** specify the type of commerce, specifically a type of commerce which may be regulated by Congress, in which the goods were sold or shipped, or the services were rendered. (See page 2 for a discussion of the meaning of "use in commerce.") For example, indicate "interstate commerce" (commerce between two or more states) or commerce between the United States and a specific foreign country, for example, "commerce between the U.S. and Canada."

In the **third blank** specify the date that the mark was first used anywhere to identify the goods or services specified in the application. This date will be the same as the date of first use in commerce unless the applicant made some use, for example, within a single state, before the first use in commerce.

8

In the **fourth blank** specify how the mark is placed on the goods or used with the services. This is referred to as the "method-of-use clause," and should not be confused with the identification of the goods and services described under Space 6. For example, in relation to goods, state "the mark is used on labels affixed to the goods," or "the mark is used on containers for the goods," whichever is accurate. In relation to services, state "the mark is used in advertisements for the services."

Space 7(b)

If the applicant has a bona fide intention to use the mark in commerce in relation to the goods or services specified in the application, check this second box and fill in the blank. The applicant should check this box if the mark has not been used at all or if the mark has been used on the specified goods or services only within a single state.

In the blank, state how the mark is intended to be placed on the goods or used with the services. For example, for goods, state "the mark will be used on labels affixed to the goods," or "the mark will be used on containers for the goods," whichever is accurate. For services, state "the mark will be used in advertisements for the services."

Spaces 7(c) and (d)

These spaces are usually used only by applicants from foreign countries who are filing in the United States under international agreements. These applications are less common. For further information about treaty-based applications, call the trademark information number listed in this booklet on page 5, or contact a private attorney.

Space 8 — Verification and Signature

The applicant must verify the truth and accuracy of the information in the application and must sign the application. The declaration in Space 8, on the back of the form, is for this purpose. If the application is not signed, the application will not be granted a filing date and will be returned to the applicant. If the application is not signed by an appropriate person, the application will be found void and the filing fee will be forfeited. Therefore, it is important that the proper person sign the application.

Who should sign?

- If the applicant is an **individual,** that **individual** must sign.

- If the applicant is a **partnership,** a **general partner** must sign.

- If the applicant is a **corporation, association or similar organization,** an **officer** of the corporation, association or organization must sign. An officer is a person who holds an office established in the articles of incorporation or the bylaws. **Officers may not delegate this authority to non-officers.**

- If the applicants are **joint applicants** (such as a husband and wife, or two or more people who are not engaged in any formal business relationship but who each own the mark equally) then all joint applicants must sign.

The person who signs the application must indicate the date signed, provide a telephone number to be used if it is necessary to contact the applicant, and clearly print or type their name and position.

2. THE DRAWING PAGE
Every application must include a single drawing page. If there is no drawing page, the application will be denied a filing date and returned to the applicant. The PTO uses the drawing to file the mark in the PTO search records and to print the mark in the Official Gazette and on the registration.

The drawing must be on pure white, durable, non-shiny paper that is 8½ (21.59 cm) inches wide by 11 (27.94 cm) inches long. There must be at least a one-inch (2.54 cm) margin on the sides, top and bottom of the page, and at least one inch between the heading and the display of the mark.

At the top of the drawing there must be a **heading,** listing on separate lines, the applicant's complete name, address, the goods and services specified in the application, and in applications based on use in commerce, the date of first use of the mark and the date of first use of the mark in commerce. This heading should be typewritten. If the drawing is in special form, the heading should include a description of the essential elements of the mark.

The **drawing of the mark** should appear at the center of the page. The drawing of the mark may be **typewritten,** as shown on page 20, or it may be in **special form,** as shown on page 21.

If the mark includes words, numbers or letters, the applicant can usually elect to submit either a typewritten or a special-form drawing. To register a mark consisting of only words, letters or numbers, without indicating any particular style or design, provide a typewritten drawing. In a typewritten drawing the mark must be typed entirely in **CAPITAL LET- TERS,** even if the mark, as used, includes lower-case letters. Use a standard typewriter or type of the same size and style as that on a standard typewriter.

To register a word mark in the form in which it is actually used or intended to be used in commerce, or any mark including a design, submit a **special-form** drawing. In a special-form drawing, the mark must not be larger than 4 inches by 4 inches (10.16 cm by 10.16 cm). If the drawing of the mark is larger than 4 inches by 4 inches, the application will be denied a filing date and returned to the applicant. In addition, the drawing must appear only in black and white, with every line and letter black and clear. **No color or gray shading is allowed. Do not combine typed matter and special form in the same drawing.**

The drawing in special form must be a substantially exact representation of the mark as it appears on the specimens. The applicant may apply to register any portion of a mark consisting of more than one element, provided the mark displayed in the drawing creates a separate impression apart from other elements that appear on the specimens. Generally, it is possible to register a word mark by itself even though

the specimen shows the word mark used in combination with a design or as part of a logo. Do not include non-trademark matter in the drawing, such as informational matter like "12 Fl. Oz." or "Made in U.S.A." which may appear on a label. In the end, the applicant must decide exactly what to register and in what form. The PTO considers the drawing controlling in determining exactly what mark the application covers.

Be careful in preparing the drawing. While it may be possible to make some minor changes, the rules prohibit any material change to the drawing of the mark after filing.

How to Use Color Lining

A plain black-and-white drawing is acceptable even if the mark is used in color. Most drawings do not indicate specific colors. However, some applicants may desire to claim a color or colors as part of the mark. Since all marks which are published in the Official Gazette (and printed on certificates of registration) are printed in black and white, the PTO has adopted standard color lining codes, shown below, which are to be used when color is claimed as a feature of a mark. For example, if the mark is a five-point star, an applicant could draw horizontal lines (the lining code for the color blue) through the star to indicate that not only is the mark a five-point star, but it is a blue five-point star. Without a lining code in the mark, then the registration would be for a five-point star in any color.

To indicate color, use the color linings shown below. The appropriate lining should appear in the area where the relevant color would appear. If the drawing is lined for color, insert a statement in the written application to so indicate, for example, "The mark is lined for the colors red and green." The PTO has adopted eight standard lining codes. If a mark is a particular shade of blue, for example "sky blue," use the blue lining code and indicate in the color lining statement that the mark is "sky blue." The sample special form drawing on page 21 shows how to use color lining in a drawing. In the sample, the word "Pinstripes" is superimposed over a red background. The vertical lines shown in the rectangle is the lining code for the color red. If the applicant did not want

10

to claim color as part of the mark, the applicant could simply draw a single line rectangle around the words and leave the background space inside the rectangle white (or the rectangle could be shaded black with white lettering).

If a drawing is lined for color, then the specimens submitted with the application or declaration of use **must** show the mark in the color shown on the drawing. If the drawing is not lined for color, then the mark on the specimens may appear in any color.

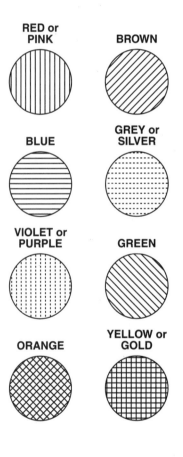

RED or PINK

BROWN

BLUE

GREY or SILVER

VIOLET or PURPLE

GREEN

ORANGE

YELLOW or GOLD

3. FEES
Filing Fee
The **application filing fee** is **$245.00** for **each class** of goods or services listed. (See the International Classification of Goods and Services on the inside back cover.) **At least $245.00 must accompany the application, or the application will be denied a filing date and all the papers returned to the applicant.** Fee increases, when necessary, usually take effect on October 1 of any given year. If filing after September 1997, please call 1-800-PTO-9199 for up-to-date fee information. The PTO receives no taxpayer funds, and all operations are supported entirely from fees paid by applicants and registrants.

Additional Fees Related to Intent-To-Use Applications
In addition to the application filing fee, applicants filing based on a bona fide intention to use a mark in commerce must submit a fee of **$100.00** for **each class** of goods or services in the application when filing any of the following:

• an AMENDMENT TO ALLEGE USE

• a STATEMENT OF USE

• a REQUEST FOR AN EXTENSION OF TIME TO FILE A STATEMENT OF USE

NOTE: FEES ARE GENERALLY NOT REFUNDABLE.

Form of Payment
All payments must be made in United States currency, by check, post office money order or certified check. Personal or business checks may be submitted. Make checks and money orders payable to: **Commissioner of Patents and Trademarks.**

4. SPECIMENS
The following information is designed to provide guidance regarding the specimens required to show use of the mark in commerce.

When to File the Specimens
If the applicant has already used the mark in commerce and files based on this use in commerce, then

the applicant must submit **three specimens per class** showing use of the mark in commerce with the application. If, instead, the application is based on a bona fide intention to use mark in commerce, the applicant must submit **three specimens per class** at the time the applicant files either an AMENDMENT TO ALLEGE USE or a STATEMENT OF USE.

What to File as a Specimen
The specimens must be actual samples of how the mark is being used in commerce. **The specimens may be identical or they may be examples of three different uses showing the same mark.**

If the mark is used on **goods,** examples of acceptable specimens are tags or labels which are attached to the goods, containers for the goods, displays associated with the goods, or photographs of the goods showing use of the mark on the goods themselves. If it is impractical to send an actual specimen because of its size, photographs or other acceptable reproductions that show the mark on the goods, or packaging for the goods, must be furnished. *Invoices, announcements, order forms, bills of lading, leaflets, brochures, catalogs, publicity releases, letterhead, and business cards generally **are not acceptable** specimens for goods.*

If the mark is used for **services,** examples of acceptable specimens are signs, brochures about the services, advertisements for the services, business cards or stationery showing the mark in connection with the services, or photographs which show the mark either as it is used in the rendering or advertising of the services. In the case of a service mark, the specimens must either show the mark and include some clear reference to the type of services rendered under the mark in some form of advertising, or show the mark as it is used in the rendering of the service, for example on a store front or the side of a delivery or service truck. If business cards or *blank business letterhead* are submitted, the mark itself must make some reference to the services. For example a business card or blank letterhead which shows the mark "Joe's Real Estate" for a real estate agency *would be acceptable.* If, however, the mark is "XYZ" for a real estate agency and business cards or letterhead are submitted which do not refer to or show some con-

nection real estate services, then the blank business letterhead or business card which simply contains "XYZ" and a person's name and address *would not be acceptable.* Copies of letters *actually written* on "XYZ" business letterhead which refer to the services offered *would be acceptable.*

Specimens may not be larger than 8½ inches by 11 inches (21.59 cm by 27.94 cm) and must be flat. See pages 22 through 24 for samples of some different types of specimens. Smaller specimens, such as labels, may be stapled to a sheet of paper and labeled "SPECIMENS." A separate sheet can be used for each class.

ADDITIONAL REQUIREMENTS FOR INTENT-TO-USE APPLICATIONS -
An applicant who files its application based on a bona fide intention to use a mark in commerce *must make use of the mark in commerce before the mark can register.* After use in commerce begins, the applicant must submit:

1. three specimens evidencing use as discussed above;

2. a fee of **$100.00** per class of goods or services in the application; and

3. **either** (1) an AMENDMENT TO ALLEGE USE if the application has not yet been approved for publication **or** (2) a STATEMENT OF USE if the mark has been published and the PTO has issued a NOTICE OF ALLOWANCE.

The same form, PTO Form 1553, entitled "ALLEGATION OF USE FOR INTENT-TO-USE APPLICATIONS, WITH DECLARATION," can be used to file either an AMENDMENT TO ALLEGE USE or a STATEMENT OF USE.

The AMENDMENT TO ALLEGE USE is the form which is filed **BEFORE** an applicant has had its intent-to-use application approved by an Examining Attorney for publication in the Official Gazette. If an AMENDMENT TO ALLEGE USE is filed between the date the mark is approved for publication and the date of issuance of the NOTICE OF ALLOWANCE, the papers and filing fee will be returned to the applicant unprocessed.

The STATEMENT OF USE is the form which is filed **AFTER** an applicant receives its NOTICE OF ALLOWANCE. Please do not file this form before receiving the NOTICE OF ALLOWANCE, or the form will not be accepted. The NOTICE OF ALLOWANCE will not be sent to an applicant until: (1) the application has been approved by the Examining Attorney; (2) the mark has been published in the Official Gazette; and (3) no Notice of Opposition has been filed by a third party within 30 days of the date of publication of the mark in the Official Gazette.

If the applicant will not make use of the mark in commerce within six months of the date of issuance of the NOTICE OF ALLOWANCE, **the applicant must file** a REQUEST FOR AN EXTENSION OF TIME TO FILE A STATEMENT OF USE, or the application **is abandoned.** (Use PTO Form 1581, which is intended only for this purpose.) The fee for filing a REQUEST FOR AN EXTENSION OF TIME TO FILE A STATEMENT OF USE is $100 per class of goods or services.

See the instructions and information on the back of the forms. The information about specimens on pages 11 and 12 of this booklet, and about and dates of use on page 8, is also relevant to filing an AMENDMENT TO ALLEGE USE or STATE-MENT OF USE. Follow the instructions on these forms carefully. Failure to file the necessary papers in proper form within the time provided may result in abandonment of the application.

PATENT AND TRADEMARK OFFICE SERVICES

Trademark Assistance Center

In order to provide improved service to trademark applicants, registrants, and the general public, the Patent and Trademark Office has implemented a pilot program called the "Trademark Assistance Center." The Center provides general information about the trademark registration process and responds to inquiries pertaining to the status of specific trademark applications and registrations. The location of the Center is 2900 Crystal Drive, Room 4B10, Arlington, Virginia 22202-3513. Assistance may be obtained in-person or by dialing (703) 308-9000, Monday through Friday, 8:30 a.m.-5:00 p.m. eastern time, except holidays. Please note that assistance concerning trademark and patent matters is also available at (703) 308-HELP or 1-800-PTO-9199, and that recorded information is available at (703) 557-INFO. Also, automated information about the status of trademark applications and registrations is available at (703) 305-8747.

Patent and Trademark Office on the Internet

For applicants who have access to a personal computer with a World Wide Web browser, the PTO does have a site on the Internet at http://www.uspto.gov/.

Trademark information available on the PTO home-page includes *Basic Facts About Trademarks* booklet, along with the forms in this booklet. Also offered are current fee schedules; fact sheets, the *Trademark Manual of Acceptable Identifications and Classifications for Goods and Services, and Trademark Trial and Appeal Board Manual of Procedure.* The *Trademark Manual of Acceptable Identifications and Classifications for Goods and Services* has thousands of listings for goods and services which the PTO routinely accepts, along with the proper International Classification for the goods or services. Applicants are encouraged to use this resource in drafting identifications for goods and services. The PTO homepage is formatted in Word Perfect 5.1 for Windows (convertible to Word) and in Pagemaker 5.0.

Please note that although the PTO has a homepage on the Internet, **the PTO is not presently accepting electronically filed applications.** Do not attempt to send trademark applications electronically to the Office. They will not be accepted or processed.

Patent and Trademark Depository Libraries

The following libraries, designated as Patent and Trademark Depository Libraries (PTDL's) receive patent and trademark information in various formats from the U.S. Patent and Trademark Office. Many PTDL's have on file all full-text patents issued since 1790, trademarks published since 1872, and selected collections of foreign patents. All PTDL's have both the patent and trademark sections of the *Official*

Gazette of the U.S. Patent and Trademark Office. The full-text utility and design patents are distributed numerically on 16 mm microfilm, and plant patents on color microfiche. Patent and trademark search systems on CD-ROM format are available at all PTDL's to increase utilization of and enhance access to the information found in patents and trademarks. It is through the CD-ROM systems that preliminary patent and trademark searches can be conducted through the numerically arranged collections.

All information is available for use by the public free of charge. Facilities for making paper copies of patent and trademark information are generally provided for a fee.

Patent and Trademark Depository Libraries

State	City/Library	Telephone
Alabama	Auburn University: Ralph Brown Draughon Library	334-844-1747
	Birmingham Public Library	205-226-3620
Alaska	Anchorage: Z.J. Loussac Public Library	907-562-7323
Arizona	Tempe: Daniel E. Nobel Science and Engineering Library,	
	Arizona State University	602-965-7010
Arkansas	Little Rock: Arkansas State Library	501-682-2053
California	Los Angeles Public Library	213-228-7220
	Sacramento: California State Library	916-654-0069
	San Diego Public Library	619-236-5813
	San Francisco Public Library	415-557-4500
	*Sunnyvale Center for Innovation, Invention and Ideas	**408-730-7290**
Colorado	Denver Public Library	303-640-6220
Connecticut	New Haven: Science Park Patent Library	203-786-5447
Delaware	Newark: University of Delaware Library	302-831-2965
District of Columbia	Washington: Founders Library, Howard University	202-806-7252
Florida	Fort Lauderdale: Broward County Main Library	954-357-7444
	Miami-Dade Public Library	305-375-2665
	Orlando: University of Central Florida Libraries	407-823-2562
	Tampa Campus Library, University of South Florida	813-974-2726
Georgia	Atlanta: Price Gilvert Memorial Library Georgia Institute of Technology	404-894-4508
Hawaii	Honolulu: Hawaii State Public Library System	808-586-3477
Idaho	Moscow: University of Idaho Library	208-885-6235
Illinois	Chicago Public Library	312-747-4450
	Springfield: Illinois State Library	217-782-5659
Indiana	Indianapoli—Marion County Public Library	317-269-1741
	West Lafayette: Siegesmund Engineering Library, Purdue University	317-494-2872

State	City/Library	Telephone
Iowa	Des Moines: State Library of Iowa	515-281-4118
Kansas	Wichita: Abla Library, Wichita State University	316-978-3155
Kentucky	Louisville Free Public Library	502-574-1611
Louisana	Baton Rouge: Troy H. Middleton Library, Louisana State University	504-388-5652
Maine	Orono: Raymond H. Fogler Library, University of Maine	207-581-1678
Maryland	College Park: Engineering and Physical Sciences Library, University of Maryland	310-405-9157
Massachusetts	Amherst: Physical Sciences Library, University of Massachusetts Boston Public Library	413-545-1370 617-536-5400 ext. 265
Michigan	Ann Arbor: Engineering Library, University of Michigan Big Rapids: Abigail S. Timme Library, Ferris State University ***Detroit: Great Lakes Patent and Trademark Center, Detroit Public Library**	313-647-5735 616-592-3602 **313-833-3379**
Minnesota	Minneapolis Public Library and Information Center	612-372-6570
Mississippi	Jackson: Mississippi Library Commission	601-359-1036
Missouri	Kansas City: Linda Hall Library St. Louis Public Library	816-363-4600 314-241-2288 ext. 390
Montana	Butte: Montana Tech of the University of Montana Library	406-496-4281
Nebraska	Lincoln: Engineering Library, University of Nebraska-Lincoln	402-472-3411
Nevada	Reno: University of Nevada-Reno Library	702-784-6579 ext. 257
New Hampshire	Concord: New Hampshire State Library	603 271-2239
New Jersey	Newark Public Library Piscataway: Library of Science and Medicine, Rutgers University	201-733-7782 908-445-2895
New Mexico	Albuquerque: Centennial Science and Engineering Library, University of New Mexico	505-277-4412
New York	Albany: New York State Library Buffalo and Erie County Public Library New York Public Library, Science, Industry and Business Library	518-474-5355 716-858-7101 212-592-7000
North Carolina	Raleigh: D.H. Hill Library, North Carolina State University	919-515-3280
North Dakota	Grand Forks: Chester Fritz Library, University of North Dakota	701-777-4888
Ohio	Akron-Summit County Public Library Cincinnati and Hamilton County, the Public Library of Cleveland Public Library Columbus: Ohio State University Libraries Toledo/Lucas County Public Library	330-643-9075 513-369-6936 216-623-2870 614-292-6175 419-259-5212
Oklahoma	Stillwater: Center for International Trade Development, Oklahoma State University	405-744-7086
Oregon	Portland: Paul L. Boley Law Library, Lewis & Clark College	503-768-6786
Pennsylvania	Philadelphia, The Free Library of Pittsburgh, the Carnegie Library of University Park: Pattee Library, Pennsylvania State University	215-686-5331 412-622-3138 814-865-4861
Puerto Rico	Mayaguez: General Library, University of Puerto Rico—Mayaguez	787-832-4040 ext. 4359
Rhode Island	Providence Public Library	401-455-8027
South Carolina	Clemson: R. M. Cooper Library, Clemson University	864-656-3024
South Dakota	Rapid City: Devereaux Library, South Dakota School of Mines and Technology	605-394-6822

State	City/Library	Telephone
Tennessee	Memphis & Shelby County Public Library and Information Center	901-725-8877
	Nashville: Styevenson Science and Engineering Library,	
	Vanderbilt University	615-322-2717
Texas	Austin: McKinney Engineering Library, University of Texas at Austin	512-495-4500
	College Station: Sterling C. Evans Library, Texas A&M University	409-845-3826
	Dallas Public Library	214-670-1468
	Houston: The Fondren Library, Rice University	713-527-8101 ext. 2587
	Lubbock: Texas Tech University Library	Not yet operational
Utah	Salt Lake City: Marriott Library, University of Utah	801-581-8394
Virginia	Richmond: James Branch Cabell Library, Virginia	
	Commonwealth University	804-828-1104
Washington	Seattle: Engineering Library, University of Washington	206-543-0740
West Virginia	Morgantown: Evansdale Library, West Virginia University	304-293-2510 ext. 113
Wisconsin	Madison: Kurt F. Wendt Library, University of Wisconsin-Madison	608-262-6845
	Milwaukee Public Library	414-286-3051
Wyoming	Casper: Natrona County Public Library	307-237-4935

Sample Applications
Sample Drawings
Sample Specimens
Application Forms and Instructions

®

SAMPLE WRITTEN APPLICATION
BASED ON INTENT TO USE IN COMMERCE
(One class)

TRADEMARK/SERVICE MARK APPLICATION, PRINCIPAL REGISTER, WITH DECLARATION	MARK (Word(s) and/or Design) PINSTRIPES and design	1	CLASS NO. (If known) 16 & 35	2

TO THE ASSISTANT COMMISSIONER FOR TRADEMARKS:

APPLICANT'S NAME: Pinstripes Inc. **3**

APPLICANT'S MAILING ADDRESS: 100 Main Street **4**

(Display address exactly as it should appear on registration)   Anytown, Missouri   12345

APPLICANT'S ENTITY TYPE: (Check one and supply requested information)

Individual - Citizen of (Country):	**5a**
Partnership - State where organized (Country, if appropriate): _____ Names and Citizenship (Country) of General Partners:	**5b**
Corporation - State (Country, if appropriate) of Incorporation:	**5c**
Other (Specify Nature of Entity and Domicile):	**5d**

GOODS AND/OR SERVICES:

Applicant requests registration of the trademark/service mark shown in the accompanying drawing in the United States Patent and Trademark Office on the Principal Register established by the Act of July 5, 1946 (15 U.S.C. 1051 et. seq., as amended) for the following goods/services **(SPECIFIC GOODS AND/OR SERVICES MUST BE INSERTED HERE):**

Magazines in the field of business management (Class 16); **6**
Business management consulting services (Class 35)

BASIS FOR APPLICATION: (Check boxes which apply, but never both the first AND second boxes, and supply requested information related to each box checked.)

[x] 7a	Applicant is using the mark in commerce on or in connection with the above identified goods/services. (15 U.S.C. 1051(a), as amended.) Three specimens showing the mark as used in commerce are submitted with this application. • Date of first use of the mark in commerce which the U.S. Congress may regulate (for example, interstate or between the U.S. and a foreign country): (Class 16) 1/15/92; (Class 35) 8/27/90 • Specify the type of commerce: interstate (for example, interstate or between the U.S. and a specified foreign country) • Date of first use anywhere (the same as or before use in commerce date): Cl 16-1/15/92; Cl 35-8/27/90 • Specify intended manner or mode of use of mark on or in connection with the goods/services: _____ On the magazines and in advertisements for the services (for example, trademark is applied to labels, service mark is used in advertisements)
[ ] 7b	Applicant has a bona fide intention to use the mark in commerce on or in connection with the above identified goods/services. (15 U.S.C. 1051(b), as amended.) • Specify manner or mode of use of mark on or in connection with the goods/services: _____ (for example, trademark will be applied to labels, service mark will be used in advertisements)
[ ] 7c	Applicant has a bona fide intention to use the mark in commerce on or in connection with the above identified goods/services, and asserts a claim of priority based upon a foreign application in accordance with 15 U.S.C. 1126(d), as amended. • Country of foreign filing: _____ • Date of foreign filing: _____
[ ] 7d	Applicant has a bona fide intention to use the mark in commerce on or in connection with the above identified goods/services and, accompanying this application, submits a certification or certified copy of a foreign registration in accordance with 15 U.S.C 1126(e), as amended. • Country of registration: _____ • Registration number: _____

NOTE: Declaration, on Reverse Side, MUST be Signed

... like so made are punishable ... ful false statements may ... res that he/she is properly ... ieves the applicant to be the ... ication is being filed under 15 ... rk in commerce; to the best of ... tion has the right to use the ... n such near resemblance thereto as to be likely, when used on or in connection with the goods/services of such other person, to cause confusion, or to cause mistake, or to deceive; and that all statements made of his/her own knowledge are true and that all statements made on information and belief are believed to be true.

November 21, 1996	*John Doe, Jr.*
DATE	SIGNATURE
(123) 456-7890	John Doe, Jr., President
TELEPHONE NUMBER	PRINT OR TYPE NAME AND POSITION

18

SAMPLE WRITTEN APPLICATION BASED ON USE IN COMMERCE
(Two classes)

TRADEMARK/SERVICE MARK APPLICATION, PRINCIPAL REGISTER, WITH DECLARATION	MARK (Word(s) and/or Design) THEORYTEC	1	CLASS NO. (If known) 9	2

TO THE ASSISTANT COMMISSIONER FOR TRADEMARKS:

APPLICANT'S NAME: A-OK Software Development Group   **3**

APPLICANT'S MAILING ADDRESS: **4**
100 Main Street
(Display address exactly as it should appear on registration)   Anytown, Missouri 12345

APPLICANT'S ENTITY TYPE: (Check one and supply requested information)

Individual - Citizen of (Country):	**5a**
Partnership - State where organized (Country, if appropriate): __Missouri__ Names and Citizenship (Country) of General Partners: _Mary Baker, citizen of the USA;_ _Harry Parker, citizen of the USA; and Jane Witlow, citizen of the USA_	**5b**
Corporation - State (Country, if appropriate) of Incorporation:	**5c**
Other (Specify Nature of Entity and Domicile):	**5d**

GOODS AND/OR SERVICES:

Applicant requests registration of the trademark/service mark shown in the accompanying drawing in the United States Patent and Trademark Office on the Principal Register established by the Act of July 5, 1946 (15 U.S.C. 1051 et. seq., as amended) for the following goods/services (**SPECIFIC GOODS AND/OR SERVICES MUST BE INSERTED HERE**):

Computer software for analyzing sales statistics for retail stores   **6**

BASIS FOR APPLICATION: (Check boxes which apply, but never both the first AND second boxes, and supply requested information related to each box checked.)

[ ]
 7a
	Applicant is using the mark in commerce on or in connection with the above identified goods/services. (15 U.S.C. 1051(a), as amended.) Three specimens showing the mark as used in commerce are submitted with this application.
	 • Date of first use of the mark in commerce which the U.S. Congress may regulate (for example, interstate or between the U.S. and a foreign country): _____
	 • Specify the type of commerce: _____
	   (for example, interstate or between the U.S. and a specified foreign country)
	 • Date of first use anywhere (the same as or before use in commerce date): _____
	 • Specify intended manner or mode of use of mark on or in connection with the goods/services: _____
	   (for example, trademark is applied to labels, service mark is used in advertisements)

x[x]x
 7b
	Applicant has a bona fide intention to use the mark in commerce on or in connection with the above identified goods/services. (15 U.S.C. 1051(b), as amended.)
	 • Specify manner or mode of use of mark on or in connection with the goods/services: __On labels__
	   affixed to the software
	   (for example, trademark will be applied to labels, service mark will be used in advertisements)

[ ] 7c	Applicant has a bona fide intention to use the mark in commerce on or in connection with the above identified goods/services, and asserts a claim of priority based upon a foreign application in accordance with 15 U.S.C. 1126(d), as amended. • Country of foreign filing: _____ • Date of foreign filing: _____
[ ] 7d	Applicant has a bona fide intention to use the mark in commerce on or in connection with the above identified goods/services and, accompanying this application, submits a certification or certified copy of a foreign registration in accordance with 15 U.S.C 1126(e), as amended. • Country of registration: _____ • Registration number: _____

NOTE: Declaration, on Reverse Side, MUST be Signed

like so made are punishable lful false statements may ares that he/she is properly lieves the applicant to be the lication is being filed under 15 rk in commerce; to the best of ation has the right to use the in such near resemblance thereto as to be likely, when used on or in connection with the goods/services of such other person, to cause confusion, or to cause mistake, or to deceive; and that all statements made of his/her own knowledge are true and that all statements made on information and belief are believed to be true.

____November 19, 1996____
DATE

(123) 456-7890

_____
TELEPHONE NUMBER

Mary Baker
SIGNATURE
Mary Baker, General Partner

_____
PRINT OR TYPE NAME AND POSITION

SAMPLE DRAWING–TYPEWRITTEN

8½" x 11" (21.6 cm x 27.9 cm)

APPLICANT'S NAME: A-OK Software Development Group

APPLICANT'S ADDRESS: 100 Main Street, Any town, MO 12345

GOODS: Computer software for analyzing sales statistics for retail stores.

DATE OF FIRST USE: Intent-to-Use Application

DATE OF FIRST USE IN COMMERCE: Intent-to-Use Application

THEORYTEC

20

SAMPLE DRAWING–SPECIAL FORM

8½" x 11" (21.6 cm x 27.9 cm)

APPLICANT'S NAME: Pinstripes Inc.

APPLICANT"S ADDRESS: 100 Main Street, Any town, MO 12345

GOODS AND SERVICES: Magazines in the field of business
management; business management
consulting services

FIRST USE: Magazines (Class 16) January 15, 1992
Consulting (Class 35) August 27, 1990

FIRST USE IN COMMERCE: Magazines (Class 16) January 15, 1992
Consulting (Class 35) August 27, 1990

DESIGN: A zebra

LINING: The mark is lined for the color red.

21

SAMPLE SPECIMENS FOR GOODS
(Label affixed to computer disc)

SAMPLE SPECIMEN FOR SERVICES (Advertisement)

If better business management solutions are what you're after, then think of **Pinstripes** for consulting. We'll come wherever you are to offer a wide range of consulting services for diverse industries, including high-tech fields. You'll like the results, as well as our competitive price.

The more you get to know us, the more you'll realize that we're a best choice for consulting that can make a big difference. Call or write us.

Pinstripes Inc.
(123) 456-7890
100 Main St., Any town, MO 12345

SAMPLE SPECIMEN FOR SERVICES
(Business card showing mark <u>and</u> reference to service)

BUSINESS MANAGEMENT CONSULTANTS

John Doe, *President*

100 Main Street
Any town, MO 12345 U.S.A.
(123) 456-7890

23

®

SAMPLE SPECIMEN FOR GOODS (Issue of Magazine)

If the rectangle shown in the drawing **is not lined for color.** i.e.. shaded black with white letters, or black letters on a white background, **then specimens showing the mark in any color (or in black and white) are acceptable.** If the rectangle is lined for color, *e.g., red,* then the background around the word "Pinstripes" **must be red** in order for the specimen to be acceptable.

April — May 1992 $2.00

PINSTRIPES

PINSTRIPES

"The Magazine for the Business Professional"

IN THIS ISSUE

- Managing business in tough times.

- The need for quality in everything redefines priorities.

- Managing turned inside out.

- Employee ideas can really count.

- Our business report on Washington, D.C.

- Working together to create new markets and new jobs.

- In business to stay.

- Investing feature: future outlook on futures.

- "Pinstripes forever" (our humor column).

24

TRADEMARK/SERVICE MARK APPLICATION, PRINCIPAL REGISTER, WITH DECLARATION	MARK (Word(s) and/or Design)	CLASS NO. (If known)

TO THE ASSISTANT COMMISSIONER FOR TRADEMARKS:

APPLICANT'S NAME:

APPLICANT'S MAILING ADDRESS:

(Display address exactly as it should appear on registration)

APPLICANT'S ENTITY TYPE: (**Check one** and supply requested information)

Individual - Citizen of (Country):

Partnership - State where organized (Country, if appropriate): _____
Names and Citizenship (Country) of General Partners: _____

Corporation - State (Country, if appropriate) of Incorporation: _____

Other (Specify Nature of Entity and Domicile):

GOODS AND/OR SERVICES:

Applicant requests registration of the trademark/service mark shown in the accompanying drawing in the United States Patent and Trademark Office on the Principal Register established by the Act of July 5, 1946 (15 U.S.C. 1051 et. seq., as amended) for the following goods/services (**SPECIFIC GOODS AND/OR SERVICES MUST BE INSERTED HERE**):

BASIS FOR APPLICATION: (Check boxes which apply, **but never both the first AND second boxes**, and supply requested information related to each box checked.)

[ ] Applicant is using the mark in commerce on or in connection with the above identified goods/services. (15 U.S.C. 1051(a), as amended.) Three specimens showing the mark as used in commerce are submitted with this application.
- Date of first use of the mark in commerce which the U.S. Congress may regulate (for example, interstate or between the U.S. and a foreign country): _____
- Specify the type of commerce: _____
  (for example, interstate or between the U.S. and a specified foreign country)
- Date of first use anywhere (the same as or before use in commerce date): _____
- Specify intended manner or mode of use of mark on or in connection with the goods/services: _____

  (for example, trademark is applied to labels, service mark is used in advertisements)

[ ] Applicant has a bona fide intention to use the mark in commerce on or in connection with the above identified goods/services. (15 U.S.C. 1051(b), as amended.)
- Specify manner or mode of use of mark on or in connection with the goods/services: _____

  (for example, trademark will be applied to labels, service mark will be used in advertisements)

[ ] Applicant has a bona fide intention to use the mark in commerce on or in connection with the above identified goods/services, and asserts a claim of priority based upon a foreign application in accordance with 15 U.S.C. 1126(d), as amended.
- Country of foreign filing: _____ • Date of foreign filing: _____

[ ] Applicant has a bona fide intention to use the mark in commerce on or in connection with the above identified goods/services and, accompanying this application, submits a certification or certified copy of a foreign registration in accordance with 15 U.S.C 1126(e), as amended
- Country of registration: _____ • Registration number: _____

NOTE: Declaration, on Reverse Side, MUST be Signed

DECLARATION

The undersigned being hereby warned that willful false statements and the like so made are punishable by fine or imprisonment, or both, under 18 U.S.C. 1001, and that such willful false statements may jeopardize the validity of the application or any resulting registration, declares that he/she is properly authorized to execute this application on behalf of the applicant; he/she believes the applicant to be the owner of the trademark/service mark sought to be registered, or if the application is being filed under 15 U.S.C. 1051(b), he/she believes the applicant to be entitled to use such mark in commerce; to the best of his/her knowledge and belief no other person, firm, corporation, or association has the right to use the above identified mark in commerce, either in the identical form thereof or in such near resemblance thereto as to be likely, when used on or in connection with the goods/services of such other person, to cause confusion, or to cause mistake, or to deceive; and that all statements made of his/her own knowledge are true and that all statements made on information and belief are believed to be true.

_____
DATE

_____
SIGNATURE

_____
TELEPHONE NUMBER

_____
PRINT OR TYPE NAME AND POSITION

INSTRUCTIONS AND INFORMATION FOR APPLICANT

TO RECEIVE A FILING DATE, THE APPLICATION <u>MUST</u> BE COMPLETED AND SIGNED BY THE APPLICANT AND SUBMITTED ALONG WITH:

1. The prescribed **FEE ($245.00)** for each class of goods/services listed in the application;
2. A **DRAWING PAGE** displaying the mark in conformance with 37 CFR 2.52;
3. If the application is based on use of the mark in commerce, **THREE (3) SPECIMENS** (evidence) of the mark as used in commerce for each class of goods/services listed in the application. All three specimens may be the same. Examples of good specimens include: (a) labels showing the mark which are placed on the goods; (b) photographs of the mark as it appears on the goods, (c) brochures or advertisements showing the mark as used in connection with the services.
4. An **APPLICATION WITH DECLARATION** (this form) - The application must be signed in order for the application to receive a filing date. Only the following persons may sign the declaration, depending on the applicant's legal entity: (a) the individual applicant; (b) an officer of the corporate applicant; (c) one general partner of a partnership applicant; (d) all joint applicants.

SEND APPLICATION FORM, DRAWING PAGE, FEE, AND SPECIMENS (IF APPROPRIATE) TO:

Assistant Commissioner for Trademarks
Box New App/Fee
2900 Crystal Drive
Arlington, VA 22202-3513

Additional information concerning the requirements for filing an application is available in a booklet entitled **Basic Facts About Registering a Trademark,** which may be obtained by writing to the above address or by calling: (703) 308-HELP.

This form is estimated to take an average of 1 hour to complete, including time required for reading and understanding instructions, gathering necessary information, recordkeeping, and actually providing the information. Any comments on this form, including the amount of time required to complete this form, should be sent to the Office of Management and Organization, U.S. Patent and Trademark Office, U.S. Department of Commerce, Washington, D.C. 20231. Do NOT send completed forms to this address.

| ALLEGATION OF USE FOR INTENT-TO-USE APPLICATION, WITH DECLARATION (Amendment To Allege Use/Statement Use) | MARK (Identify the mark) |
| | SERIAL NO. |

TO THE ASSISTANT COMMISSIONER FOR TRADEMARKS:

APPLICANT NAME:

Applicant requests registration of the above-identified trademark/service mark in the United States Patent and Trademark Office on the Principal Register established by the Act of July 5, 1946 (15 U.S.C. §1051 *et seq.*, as amended). Three specimens per class showing the mark as used in commerce and the prescribed fees are submitted with this statement.

Applicant is using the mark in commerce on or in connection with the following goods/services (CHECK ONLY ONE):

☐ (a) those in the application or Notice of Allowance; **OR**

☐ (b) those in the application or Notice of Allowance **except** (if goods/services are to be deleted, list the goods/services to be **deleted**): _____

_____

_____

Date of first use in commerce which the U.S. Congress may regulate:_____
Specify type of commerce: _____
(for example, interstate and/or commerce between the U.S. and a foreign country)
Date of first use anywhere: _____

Specify manner or mode of use of mark on or in connection with the goods/services: (for example, trademark is applied to labels, service mark is used in advertisements):_____

_____

The undersigned, being hereby warned that willful false statements and the like so made are punishable by fine or imprisonment, or both, under 18 U.S.C. §1001, and that such willful false statements may jeopardize the validity of the application or any resulting registration, declares that he/she is properly authorized to execute this Amendment to Allege Use or Statement of Use on behalf of the applicant; he/she believes the applicant to be the owner of the trademark/service mark sought to be registered; the trademark /service mark is now in use in commerce; and all statements made of his/her own knowledge are true and all statements made on information and belief are believed to be true.

_____
Date

_____
Signature

_____
Telephone Number

_____
Type or Print Name and Position

☐ **Check here if Request to Divide is being submitted with this statement** (if Applicant wishes to proceed to publication or registration with certain goods/services on or in connection with which it has used the mark in commerce and retain an active application for any remaining goods/services, a divisional application and fee are required. 37 C.F.R. §2.87)

PLEASE SEE REVERSE FOR MORE INFORMATION

U.S. Department of Commerce/Patent and Trademark Office

INSTRUCTIONS AND INFORMATION FOR APPLICANT

In an application based upon a bona fide intention to use a mark in commerce, **the Applicant must use its mark in commerce before a registration will be issued.** After use begins, the applicant must file the Allegation of Use. If the Allegation of Use is filed before the mark is approved for publication in the *Official Gazette* it is treated under the statute as **an Amendment to Allege Use (AAU).** If it is filed after the Notice of Allowance is issued, it is treated under the statute as **a Statement of Use (SOU).** The Allegation of Use cannot be filed during the time period between approval of the mark for publication in the *Official Gazette* and the issuance of the Notice of Allowance. The difference between the AAU and SOU is the time at which each is filed during the process.

Additional requirements for filing this Allegation of Use:

1) the fee of $100.00 per class of goods/services (**please note that fees are subject to change, usually on October 1 of each year**); and
2) three (3) specimens of the mark as used in commerce for each class of goods/services (for example, photographs of the mark as it appears on the goods, labels for affixation on goods, advertisements showing the mark as used in connection with services).

• The Applicant may list dates of use for one item in each class of goods/services identified in the Allegation of Use. The Applicant must have used the mark in commerce on all the goods/services in the class, however, it is only necessary to list the dates of use for one item in each class.

• Only the following persons may sign the verification on this form: (a) the individual applicant; (b) an officer of a corporate applicant; (c) one general partner of a partnership applicant; (d) all joint applicants.

• The goods/services in the Allegation of Use must be the same as those specified in the application or Notice of Allowance. The Applicant may limit or clarify the goods/services, but cannot add to or otherwise expand the identification specified in the application or Notice of Allowance. If goods/services are deleted, they may **not** be reinserted at a later time.

• Amendments to Allege Use are governed by Trademark Act §1(c), 15 U.S.C. §1051(c) and Trademark Rule 2.76, 37 C.F.R. §2.76. Statements of Use are governed by Trademark Act §1(d), 15 U.S.C. §1051(d) and Trademark Rule 2.88, 37 C.F.R. §2.88.

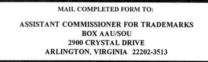

MAIL COMPLETED FORM TO:

ASSISTANT COMMISSIONER FOR TRADEMARKS
BOX AAU/SOU
2900 CRYSTAL DRIVE
ARLINGTON, VIRGINIA 22202-3513

Please note that the filing date of a document in the Patent and Trademarks Office is the date of receipt in the Office, not the date of deposit of the mail. 37 C.F.R. §1.6. To avoid lateness due to mail delay, use of the certificate of mailing set forth below, is encouraged.

COMBINED CERTIFICATE OF MAILING/CHECKLIST

Before filing this form, please make sure to complete the following:

☐ three specimens, per class have been enclosed;
☐ the filing fee of $100 (subject to change as noted above), per class has been enclosed; and
☐ the declaration has been signed by the appropriate party

CERTIFICATE OF MAILING

I do hereby certify that the foregoing are being **deposited** with the United States Postal Service as first class mail, postage prepaid, in an envelope addressed to the Assistant Commissioner for Trademarks, 2900 Crystal Drive, Arlington, VA 22202-3513, on _____ (date).

_____   _____
Signature   Date of Deposit

_____
Print or Type Name of Person Signing Certificate

This form is estimated to take 15 minutes to complete including time required for reading and understanding instructions, gathering necessary information, record keeping and actually providing the information. Any comments on the amount of time you require to complete this form should be sent to the Office of Management and Organization, U.S. Patent and Trademark Office, U.S. Department of Commerce, Washington, D.C. 20231. Do not send forms to this address.

REQUEST FOR EXTENSION OF TIME TO FILE A STATEMENT OF USE, WITH DECLARATION	MARK (Identify the mark)
	SERIAL NO.

TO THE ASSISTANT SECRETARY AND COMMISSIONER OF PATENTS AND TRADEMARKS:

APPLICANT NAME:

NOTICE OF ALLOWANCE MAILING DATE:

Applicant requests a six-month extension of time to file the Statement of Use under 37 CFR 2.89 in this application.

Applicant has a continued bona fide intention to use the mark in commerce on or in connection with the following goods/services: (Check One below)

☐ Those goods/services identified in the Notice of Allowance.

☐ Those goods/services identified in the Notice of Allowance except: (Identify goods/services to be **deleted** from application)

_____

_____

This is the _____ request for an Extension of Time following mailing of the Notice of Allowance.
    (Specify: First - Fifth)

If this is not the first request for an Extension of Time. check one box below. If the first box is checked explain the circumstance(s) of the non-use in the space provided:

☐   Applicant has not used the mark in commerce yet on all goods/services specified in the Notice of Allowance: however, applicant has made the following ongoing efforts to use the mark in commerce on or in connection with each of the goods/services specified above:

_____

If additional space is needed, please attach a separate sheet to this form

☐   Applicant believes that it has made valid use of the mark in commerce. as evidenced by the Statement of Use submitted with this request; however, if the Statement of Use does not meet minimum requirements under 37 CFR 2.88(e). applicant will need additional time in which to file a new statement.

The undersigned being hereby warned that willful false statements and the like so made are punishable by fine or imprisonment. or both, under 18 U.S.C. 1001, and that such willful false statements may jeopardize the validity of the application or any resulting registration, declares that he/she is properly authorized to execute this Request for an Extension of Time to File a Statement of Use on behalf of the applicant; and that all statements made of his/her own knowledge are true and all statements made on information and belief are believed to be true.

_____   _____
Date   Signature

_____   _____
Telephone Number   Type or Print Name and Position

☐   **Check here if Request to Divide is being submitted with this statement** (if Applicant wishes to proceed to publication or registration with certain goods/services on or in connection with which it has used the mark in commerce and retain an active application for any remaining goods/services, a divisional application and fee are required. 37 C.F.R. §2.87)

INSTRUCTIONS AND INFORMATION FOR APPLICANT

Applicant must file a Statement of Use within six months after the mailing of the Notice of Allowance based upon a bona fide intention to use a mark in commerce, UNLESS, within that same period, applicant submits a request for a six-month extension of time to file the Statement of Use. The written request **must**:

    (1)   be received in the PTO within six months after the issue date of the Notice of Allowance,

    (2)   include applicant's verified statement of continued bona fide intention to use the mark in commerce,

    (3)   specify the goods/services to which the request pertains as they are identified in the Notice of Allowance, and

    (4)   include a fee of $100 for each class of goods/services **(please note that fees are subject to change, usually on October 1 of each year).**

Applicant may request four further six-month extensions of time. No extensions may extend beyond 36 months from the issue date of the Notice of Allowance. Each further request must be received in the PTO within the previously granted six-month extension period and must include, in addition to the above requirements, a showing of **GOOD CAUSE**. This good cause showing must include:

    (1)   applicant's statement that the mark has not been used in commerce yet on all the goods or services specified in the Notice of Allowance with which applicant has a continued bona fide intention to use the mark in commerce, **and**

    (2)   applicant's statement of ongoing efforts to make such use, which may include the following: (a) product or service research or development, (b) market research, (c) promotional activities, (d) steps to acquire distributors, (e) steps to obtain required governmental approval, or (f) similar specified activity.

Applicant may submit one additional six-month extension request during the existing period in which applicant files the Statement of Use, unless the granting of this request would extend the period beyond 36 months from the issue date of the Notice of Allowance. As a showing of good cause for such a request, applicant should state its belief that applicant has made valid use of the mark in commerce, as evidenced by the submitted Statement of Use, but that if the Statement is found by the PTO to be defective, applicant will need additional time in which to file a new statement of use.

Only the following person may sign the declaration of the Request for Extension of Time: (a) the individual applicant; (b) an officer of corporate applicant; (c) one general partner of partnership applicant; (d) all joint applicants.

MAILING INSTRUCTIONS

MAIL COMPLETED FORM TO:

ASSISTANT COMMISSIONER FOR TRADEMARKS
BOX ITU
2900 CRYSTAL DRIVE
ARLINGTON, VIRGINIA 22202-3513

Please note that the filing date of a document in the Patent and Trademarks Office is the date of receipt in the Office, not the date of deposit of the mail. 37 C.F. R. §1.6. To avoid lateness due to mail delay, use of the certificate of mailing set forth below is encouraged.

CERTIFICATE OF MAILING

I do hereby certify that this correspondence is being **deposited** with the United States Postal Service as first class mail, postage prepaid, in an envelope addressed to the Assistant Commissioner for Trademarks, 2900 Crystal Drive, Arlington, VA 22202-3513, on _____ (date).

_____
Signature

_____
Print or Type Name of Person Signing Certificate

_____
Date of Deposit

This form is estimated to take 15 minutes to complete including time required for reading and understanding instructions, gathering necessary information, record keeping and actually providing the information. Any comments on the amount of time you require to complete this form should be sent to the Office of Management and Organization, U.S. Patent and Trademark Office, U.S. Department of Commerce, Washington, D.C. 20231. Do not send forms to this address.

Trademark Processing Fees

361	2.6(a)(1)	Application for registration, per class	245.00
362	2.6(a)(2)	Filing an Amendment to Allege Use under § I(c), per class	100.00
363	2.6(a)(3)	Filing a Statement of Use under § I(d)(l), per class	100.00
364	2.6(a)(4)	Filing a Request for a Six-month Extension of Time for Filing a Statement of Use under § I(d)(l), per class	100.00
365	2.6(a)(5)	Application for renewal, per class	300.00
366	2.6(a)(6)	Additional fee for late renewal, per class	100.00
367	2.6(a)(7)	Publication of mark under §12(c), per class	100.00
368	2.6(a)(8)	Issuing new certificate of registration	100.00
369	2.6(a)(9)	Certificate of Correction, registrant's error	100.00
370	2.6(a3(10)	Filing disclaimer to registration	100.00
371	2.6(a)(11)	Filing amendment to registration	100.00
372	2.6(a)(12)	Filing § 8 affidavit, per class	100.00
373	2.6(a)(13)	Filing § 15 affidavit, per class	100.00
374	2.6(a)(14)	Filing combined §§ 8 & 15 affidavit, per class	200.00
375	2.6(a)(15)	Petition to the Commissioner	100.00
376	2.6(a)(16)	Petition for cancellation, per class	200.00
377	2.6(a)(17)	Notice of opposition, per class	200.00
378	2.6(a)(18)	Ex parte appeal, per class	100.00
379	2.6(a)(19)	Dividing an application, per new application (file wrapper) created	100.00

Trademark Service Fees

461	2.6(b)(1)(i)	Printed copy of each registered mark, regular service	3.00
462	2.6(b)(1)(ii)	Printed copy of each registered mark, overnight delivery to PTO box or overnight fax	6.00
463	2.6(b)(1)(iii)	Printed copy of each registered mark ordered via expedited mail or fax, exp. service	25.00
464	2.6(b)(4)(i)	Certified copy of registered mark, with title and/or status, regular service	10.00
465	2.6(b)(4)(ii)	Certified copy of registered mark, with title and/or status, expedited local service	20.00
466	2.6(b)(2)(i)	Certified or uncertified copy of trademark application as filed, regular service	15.00
467	2.6(b)(2)(ii)	Certified or uncertified copy of trademark application as filed, expedited local service	30.00
468	2.6(b)(3)	Certified or uncertified copy of trademark-related file wrapper and contents	50.00
469	2.6(b)(5)	Certified or uncertified copy of trademark document, unless otherwise provided	25.00
470	2.6(b)(7)	For assignment records, abstracts of title and certification per registration	25.00
475	1.19(g)	Comparing and certifying copies, per document, per copy	25.00
480	2.6(b)(9)	Self-service copy charge, per page	0.25
481	2.6(b)(6)	Recording trademark assignment, agreement or other paper, first mark per document	40.00
482	2.6(b)(6)	For second and subsequent marks in the same document	25.00
484	2.6(b)(10)	Labor charges for services, per hour or fraction thereof	30.00
485	2.6(b)(11)	Unspecified other services	AT COST
488	2.6(b)(8)	Each hour of X-SEARCH terminal session time	40.00
490	1.24	Trademark coupons	3.00

REMITTANCES FROM FOREIGN COUNTRIES MUST BE PAYABLE AND IMMEDIATELY NEGOTIABLE IN THE UNITED STATES FOR THE FULL AMOUNT OF THE FEE REQUIRED

*U.S. Government Printing Office: 1996 — 421-406/60438

International Schedule of Classes of Goods and Services

Goods

1. Chemicals used in industry, science and photography, as well as in agriculture, horticulture and forestry; unprocessed artificial resins, unprocessed plastics; manures; fire extinguishing compositions; tempering and soldering preparations; chemical substances for preserving foodstuffs; tanning substances; adhesives used in industry.

2. Paints, varnishes, lacquers; preservatives against rust and against deterioration of wood; colorants; mordants; raw natural resins; metals in foil and powder form for painters, decorators, printers, and artists.

3. Bleaching preparations and other substances for laundry use; cleaning, polishing, scouring and abrasive preparations; soaps, perfumery, essential oils, cosmetics, hair lotions; dentifrices.

4. Industrial oils and greases; lubricants; dust absorbing, wetting and binding compositions; fuels (including motor spirit) and illuminants; candles, wicks.

5. Pharmaceutical, veterinary and sanitary preparations; dietetic substances adapted for medical use, food for babies; plasters, materials for dressings; material for stopping teeth, dental wax, disinfectants; preparations for destroying vermin; fungicides, herbicides.

6. Common metals and their alloys; metal building materials; transportable buildings of metal; materials of metal for railway tracks; non-electric cables and wires of common metal; ironmongery, small items of metal hardware; pipes and tubes of metal; safes; goods of common metal not included in other classes; ores.

7. Machines and machine tools; motors and engines (except for land vehicles); machine coupling and transmission components (except for land vehicles); agricultural implements; incubators for eggs.

8. Hand tools and implements (hand operated); cutlery; side arms; razors.

9. Scientific, nautical, surveying, electric, photographic, cinematographic, optical, weighing, measuring, signalling, checking (supervision), life-saving and teaching apparatus and instruments; apparatus for recording, transmission or reproduction of sound or images; magnetic data carriers, recording discs; automatic vending machines and mechanisms for coin operated apparatus; cash registers, calculating machines, data processing equipment and computers; fire-extinguishing apparatus.

10. Surgical, medical, dental and veterinary apparatus and instruments, artificials limbs, eyes and teeth; orthopedic articles; suture materials.

11. Apparatus for lighting, heating, steam generating, cooking, refrigerating, drying, ventilating, water supply and sanitary purposes.

12. Vehicles; apparatus for locomotion by land, air, or water.

13. Firearms; ammunition and projectiles; explosives; fireworks.

14. Precious metals and their alloys and goods in precious metals or coated therewith, not included in other classes; jewellery, precious stones; horological and chronometric instruments.

15. Musical instruments.

16. Paper, cardboard and goods made from these materials, not included in other classes; printed matter; bookbinding material; photographs; stationery; adhesives for stationery or household purposes; artists' materials; paint brushes; typewriters and office requisites (except furniture); instructional and teaching material (except apparatus); playing cards; printers' type; printing blocks.

17. Rubber, gutta-percha, gum asbestos, mica and goods made from these materials and not included in other classes; plastics in extruded form for use in manufacture; packing, stopping and insulating materials; flexible pipes, not of metal.

18. Leather and imitations of leather, and goods made of these materials and not included in other classes; animal skins, hides; trunks and travelling bags; umbrellas, parasols and walking sticks; whips, harness and saddlery.

19. Building materials (non-metallic); rigid pipes for building; asphalt, pitch and bitumen; non-metallic transportable buildings; monuments, not of metal.

20. Furniture, mirrors, picture frames; goods (not included in other classes) of wood, cork, reed, cane, wicker, horn, bone, ivory, whalebone, shell, amber, mother-of-pearl, meeschaum and substitutes for all these materials, or of plastics.

21. Household or kitchen utensils and containers (not of precious metal or coated therewith); combs and sponges; brushes (except paint brushes); brush-making materials; articles for cleaning purposes; steelwool; unworked or semiworked glass (except glass used in building); glassware, porcelain and earthenware not included in other classes.

22. Ropes, string, nets, tents, awnings, tarpaulins, sails, sacks and bags (not included in other classes); padding and stuffing materials (except of rubber or plastics); raw fibrous textile materials.

23. Yarns and threads, for textile use.

24. Textiles and textile goods, not included in other classes; bed and table covers.

25. Clothing, footwear, headgear.

26. Lace and embroidery, ribbons and braid; buttons, hooks and eyes, pins and needles; artificial flowers.

27. Carpets, rugs, mats and matting, linoleum and other materials for covering existing floors; wall hangings (non-textile).

28. Games and playthings; gymnastic and sporting articles not included in other classes; decorations for Christmas trees.

29. Meat, fish, poultry and game; meat extracts; preserved, dried and cooked fruits and vegetables; jellies, jams, fruit sauces; eggs, milk and milk products; edible oils and fats.

30. Coffee, tea, cocoa, sugar, rice, tapioca, sago, artificial coffee; flour and preparations made from cereals, bread, pastry and confectionery, honey, treacle; yeast, baking-powder; salt, mustard; vinegar, sauces (condiments); spices; ice.

31. Agricultural, horticultural and forestry products and grains not included in other classes; live animals; fresh fruits and vegetables; seeds, natural plants and flowers; foodstuffs for animals, malt.

32. Beers; mineral and aerated waters and other non-alcoholic drinks; fruit drinks and fruit juices; syrups and other preparations for making beverages.

33. Alcoholic beverages (except beers).

34. Tobacco; smokers articles; matches.

Services

35. Advertising; business management; business administration; office functions.

36. Insurance; financial affairs; monetary affairs; real estate affairs.

37. Building construction; repair, installation services.

38. Telecommunications.

39. Transport; packaging and storage of goods; travel arrangement.

40. Treatment of materials.

41. Education; providing of training; entertainment; sporting and cultural activities.

42. Providing of food and drink; temporary accommodation; medical, hygienic and beauty care; veterinary and agricultural services; legal services; scientific and industrial research; computer programming; services that cannot be placed in other classes.

Glossary

actual confusion When proven in court, actual confusion is prima facie evidence that trademark infringement has occurred. Any event that demonstrates that consumers are confusing one product or service with another is proof of actual confusion; consumers' asking for one product by a name similar to that of the product they actually want or mail misdirected to a company that has a name similar to that of another company that offers similar services are examples of such events. Actual confusion proves that confusion between two marks is no longer merely a likelihood, which is the usual standard for proving trademark infringement, but has become a continuing reality. This is usually sufficient to convince any judge in a trademark infringement lawsuit that the plaintiff's rights are being infringed.

actual damages The profits a trademark infringer made by the infringement and the money the plaintiff lost because of the infringement. A court deciding a trademark infringement case may award either actual damages or statutory damages.

case law Law that originates in the decisions of courts as opposed to written laws passed by state legislatures or the U.S. Congress, which are called "statutes."

cease and desist letter A letter written by the lawyer for the plaintiff in a lawsuit telling the defendant to immediately cease certain specified actions that infringe the plaintiff's trademark and thereafter desist from any further such actions. These letters are usually the first indication that a defendant has that his or her actions may have violated the plaintiff's rights. Depending on the merits of the plaintiff's claims of infringement, a defendant will decide to comply with the plaintiff's demands and try to settle the infringement dispute out of court or to fight the plaintiff's assertions of infringement in court.

constructive notice The presumption that because a trademark registration is reflected in the records of the Trademark Office, which are public, everyone knows of the claim of trademark ownership that the registration evidences, regardless of whether any examination of those records is actually made.

contingency fee A lawyer's fee taken from an award of damages to the plaintiff. Trademark infringement suits are sometimes filed by lawyers who agree to work for a contingency fee; that is, the lawyer agrees that the fee for his or her work is to be taken from and is contingent upon an award by the court in favor of the plaintiff. If the plaintiff loses, the lawyer is not paid a fee. Usually a plaintiff is still responsible for bearing the costs of the suit, such as his or her lawyer's travel expenses, the costs of court reporters for depositions, and the fees of expert witnesses. Lawyers never agree to work on a contingency fee basis for defendants, who have no expectation of any awards.

copyright The set of exclusive rights that are granted, initially to the creators of works eligible for copyright protection, by the various copyright statutes that exist in most countries. In the United States, copyright protection begins when a work is first "fixed" in a tangible form and endures, in most cases, until fifty years after the death of the creator.

generic trademark A product or service name that is merely the generic name for the class of products or services it is being used to market. Such marks do not function as trademarks until they have gained enough fame to escape the anonymity inherent in them. That is, a generic mark does not point to one particular source for the product it names and, therefore, does not function as a true trademark. The reverse situation also occurs. That is, when a name for a product comes, through public usage, to indicate a whole class of products rather than one particular product, it is said to have lost its trademark status and to have become generic.

injunction A court order that directs the enjoined party to do something or, more typically, to cease doing something and to refrain from doing it in future. Plaintiffs in trademark infringement suits typically seek injunctions to stop defendants from continuing to infringe the plaintiff's copyrights. The scope of an injunction and whether a litigant's motion for one is granted is at the discretion of the judge who hears the suit. A temporary injunction is usually granted at the same time a suit is filed and endures only ten days. A preliminary injunction is granted by a judge after hearing arguments for and against the injunction from both the plaintiff and the defendant and usually lasts until the end of the lawsuit, when it may ripen into a permanent injunction by means of a paragraph to that effect in the judge's order rendering his or her decision.

intent-to-use application Since November of 1989, marketers may file what is called an "intent-to-use" application to register a trademark with the U.S. Patent and Trademark Office, as opposed to a "use-based" application, which was formerly the only sort of registration application that was allowed. Application for registration may be made before actual use of a new trademark, so long as the trademark owner has a "bona fide intent" to begin to use the mark in interstate commerce within six months of the date the registration application is filed. The period of time for beginning use of the mark may be extended, in six-month increments and upon making the proper filings, to a total period of thirty-six months. Registration may then be granted after use of the mark is made in interstate commerce. This system allows a company to claim ownership of a mark by filing an intent-to-use application to register it; when a second company conducts a trademark search to ascertain the availability of the mark, the first company's application will appear in the search report and warn the second company away from the mark. Further, intent-to-use applications confer one other important benefit not formerly available: when a registration is eventually granted to an intent-to-use applicant, the date the applicant filed the registration application is deemed to be the date the applicant's rights in the mark commenced. This has the effect of "backdating" the applicant's rights to a date prior to the date of actual use of the mark, which was formerly the date ownership rights commenced.

likelihood of confusion The test courts apply in determining infringing similarity between trademarks. If consumers are likely to confuse the new mark with the older, established trademark because of the similarity of the marks, gauged by comparing the appearance, sound, and meaning of the two marks, likelihood of confusion is said to exist.

overall commercial impression An important, usually determinative, factor in any evaluation of possible trademark infringement. The term refers to the whole impression created by a trademark on the consumer who encounters it in the marketplace. In a proper analysis, the two marks said to be in conflict are not dissected and their minor dissimilarities tallied and totaled; rather, the total effect the marks have on consumers who encounter them in the environments where they are sold is judged.

patent The rights granted by the federal government to the originator of a physical invention or industrial or technical process (a "utility patent") or an ornamental design for an "article of manufacture" (a "design patent"). Utility patents last seventeen years; design patents last fourteen years. A patent holder earns the exclusive right to make, use, and sell the invention for which the patent was granted. Any unauthorized manufacture, use, or sale of the patented invention within this country during the term of the patent is infringement.

secondary meaning When a trademark has become widely known through advertising and the popularity of the product or service it names, it is said to have acquired "secondary meaning." Secondary meaning is necessary for an otherwise generic or unregistrable mark to be entitled to registration on the Principal Register and to enjoy the full benefits of federal trademark registration.

service mark The Lanham Act, which is the federal statute governing unfair competition and trademarks, defines a service mark as "a mark used in the sale or advertising of services to identify the services of one person and distinguish them from the services of others." A word or symbol qualifies as a service mark when it is actually used in commerce to identify the services of one particular provider of services and when it functions to identify and distinguish those services form those of others. In this country, service mark ownership accrues by virtue of use of a service mark rather than by registration, although registration significantly enhances the rights of service mark owners. Roughly speaking, service mark owners acquire ownership of their marks commensurate with the duration and scope of their use of them. Services marks are often considered a variety of trademark and referred to as trademarks, or, simply, as "marks."

statutory damages A range of money damages the trademark statute allows courts to award a plaintiff in a trademark infringement suit instead of the money lost by the plaintiff as a result of an infringer's actions plus the actual amount by which the infringer profited from the use of the plaintiff's work. Because actual damages can be very difficult, time-consuming, expensive, or impossible to prove during infringement lawsuits, and because infringers often do not profit from their infringements, awards of statutory damages are often desirable.

trade dress The packaging and labeling of a product, including the nonfunctional aspects of the shape and design of the product itself and its container. The combination of these elements creates the whole visual image of the product encountered by consumers and can become a sort of indication of the origin of the product in the same way that trademarks do. Trade dress infringement, that is, the imitation of a product's packaging and container, is a variety of unfair competition; if a defendant's trade dress is likely to cause consumers to confuse the plaintiff's product with that of the defendant, the plaintiff's trade dress has been infringed.

trademark A word, phrase, sound, or symbol that represents in the marketplace the commercial reputation of a product or service. The Lanham Act, which is the U.S. federal statute governing unfair competition and trademarks, defines a trademark as "any word, name, symbol or device or any combination thereof adopted and used by a manufacturer or merchant to identify his goods and distinguish them from those manufactured or sold by others." A word or symbol qualifies as a trademark when it is actually used in commerce to identify the goods of a particular manufacturer or merchant and when it functions to identify and distinguish those goods from those of others. In this country, trademark ownership accrues by virtue of use of a trademark rather than by registration, although trademark registration significantly enhances the rights of trademark owners. Roughly speaking, trademark owners acquire rights in their marks commensurate with the duration and scope of their use of them.

trademark abandonment The cessation of use of a trademark by its owner, with intent to permanently cease any such use of the mark. Trademark abandonment makes a mark available for use by another marketer; however, it is dangerous to assume that a mark has been abandoned merely because is has fallen into disuse. A trademark owner may cease use of a mark for a time without abandoning it.

Trademark Dilution Act of 1995 A federal law that formalizes and makes a part of the federal trademark statute a principle of trademark law that had been available as a ground for suit in only about half the states. The act allows the owners of an existing "famous" trademark to ask the court to enjoin the use of the same mark by another company—even if there is no likelihood of confusion between the marks—on the ground that the defendant's use of the mark, even for noncompeting goods or services, "dilutes" the distinctive quality of the famous mark. "Dilution" is defined in the act as "the lessening of the capacity of a famous mark to identify and distinguish goods or services, regardless of the presence or absence of 1) competition between the owner of the famous mark and other parties, or 2) likelihood of confusion, mistake, or deception."

trademark directory A trademark directory lists trademarks that are registered and therefore already in use by someone else. Marks are listed alphabetically, according to the category of product or service they name or designate. A trademark directory is most useful in the case of marks that consist solely of words. A trademark directory only short-circuits further pursuit of unavailable marks; it cannot finally clear a mark for use. For this, a full trademark search is necessary.

trademark infringement The use of a trademark without permission of the trademark owner or the use of a trademark that is confusingly similar to a trademark owned by someone else. Trademark infringement is judged by the "sight, sound, and meaning test." That is, the new mark is compared to the established trademark for similarities of appearance, sound, and meaning. If the two marks are so similar that the average consumer is likely to confuse the products or services the marks name, or to believe that they are somehow related, the new name infringes the older mark. Intent is immaterial in evaluating most trademark infringement cases. In other words, use of a trademark that is confusingly similar to an established trademark will create problems whether or not it was an intentional effort to trade on the good commercial reputation of the established mark.

trademark licensing When a trademark owner allows another marketer of goods or services to use the trademark owner's mark, under terms and conditions specified in a written agreement and for specified products or services within a specified territory, in return for specified royalty payments.

trademark registration The registration of a claim to ownership of a trademark, made in Washington, D.C. in the U.S. Patent and Trademark Office, a division of the Department of Commerce. Trademark registration enhances the rights an owner gains by virtue of the use of a trademark but does not of itself create those rights. Among other advantages, a federal registrant is presumed to have rights in the registered mark superior to anyone else except prior users of the mark and is entitled to use the ® symbol (or another prescribed form of federal trademark notice) that signifies federal trademark registration. While it is possible to register a trademark both with the state governments in the states where it is used and in the (federal) U.S. Patent and Trademark Office if it is used in interstate or international commerce, federal registration rather than state registration is generally sought by trademark owners who can qualify for it because it confers much greater benefits than state trademark registration. The sort of federal trademark registration that bestows the full benefits of federal registration is registration on the Principal Register. However, if a mark is unable to qualify for the Principal Register, a Supplemental Register registration is also useful; most marks on the Supplemental Register are descriptive, surname, or geographic marks that do not yet function as trademarks in the eyes of the Trademark Office. Marks registered on the Supplemental Register are entitled to use the ® symbol and gain some benefits of federal registration, such as access to federal courts, and are presumed, after a period of five years, to have gained enough fame to qualify for an upgrade (upon request by the registrant) to the Principal Register. Trademark registration is difficult and usually requires the services of a lawyer experienced in trademark law, unlike copyright registration, which is usually readily granted after a registration process that is simple enough that copyright owners can usually accomplish it themselves.

trademark search A survey of data on existing trademarks performed by a trademark search service in order to clear a proposed trademark for use or, alternately, eliminate it from consideration because it is determined to infringe an established mark. Most marks are cleared for use by "full" trademark searches, which are searches of United States federal and state trademark registrations as well as of data regarding valid but unregistered marks. The results of trademark searches are reported in trademark search reports and are interpreted in trademark search opinion letters, examples of which are reproduced in the Appendix.

unfair competition Generally speaking, unfair competition is commercial competition by means that are overly aggressive or less than honest, although several forms of unfair competition can result from otherwise innocent blunders. By declaring certain actions "unfair" in commerce, the courts seek to promote both free competition and fair competition. Among the types of trademark-related commercial conduct that have been held to constitute unfair competition are: trademark infringement; trademark dilution; use of confusingly similar business names; use of confusingly similar literary titles; the unauthorized use of a distinctive literary or performing style; copying a product's trade dress and configuration; and infringement of the right of publicity. Not every action that has been or could be labeled unfair competition is codified, that is, enumerated and written down, in a statute. Judges may add to the list of "unfair" business tactics as new situations are presented that seem to them to entail overreaching by a marketer.

unregistrable trademarks Names (or design marks) for products or services that, because of certain inherent characteristics, are deemed by the U.S. trademark statute to be unworthy of registration. The ten statutory grounds for denial by the U.S. Patent and Trademark Office of an application to register a name or design as a trademark are: the mark is confusingly similar to a trademark that is already federally registered; the word or, more usually, symbol for which registration is sought does not function as a trademark, that is, does not act in the marketplace to identify the source of the goods or services to which it is applied; the mark is "immoral, deceptive, or scandalous"; the mark disparages or falsely suggests a connection with persons, institutions, beliefs, or national symbols, or brings them into contempt or disrepute; the mark consists of or simulates the flag or coat of arms or other insignia of the United States of or a state or municipality or a foreign nation; the mark is the name, portrait, or signature of a particular living individual who has not given his or her consent for use of the mark or is the name, signature, or portrait of deceased president of the United States during the life of his or her surviving spouse, unless that spouse has given consent to use of the mark; the mark is "merely descriptive" of the goods or services it names; the mark is "deceptively misdescriptive" of the goods or services it names; the mark is "primarily geo-graphically descriptive or deceptively misdescriptive" of the goods or services it names; and the mark is primarily a surname.

use-based application An application to register a trademark in the U.S. Patent and Trademark Office based on current use of the mark in interstate or international commerce. Use-based applications were once the only sort of registration application available; since a change in the law that allows registration applications based on "bona fide intent" to use the marks that are the subject of such applications, this is no longer the case.

Index

Page numbers in italics refer to sample documents.